ADVANCE ON CHAOS

PUBLISHED FOR BROWN UNIVERSITY PRESS

BY UNIVERSITY PRESS OF NEW ENGLAND

HANOVER AND LONDON, 1983

David M. La Guardia

ADVANCE ON CHAOS

The Sanctifying Imagination
of Wallace Stevens

UNIVERSITY PRESS OF NEW ENGLAND

BRANDEIS UNIVERSITY

BROWN UNIVERSITY

CLARK UNIVERSITY

DARTMOUTH COLLEGE

UNIVERSITY OF NEW HAMPSHIRE

UNIVERSITY OF RHODE ISLAND

TUFTS UNIVERSITY

UNIVERSITY OF VERMONT

Publication of this volume has been aided by a grant from the
NATIONAL ENDOWMENT FOR THE HUMANITIES.

Printed in the United States of America
Library of Congress Cataloging in Publication Data

LIBRARY OF CONGRESS CATALOGING IN PUBLICATION DATA

La Guardia, David M., 1943–
    Advance on chaos.

    Bibliography: p.
    Includes index.
    1. Stevens, Wallace, 1879–1955—Criticism and intrepre-
tation.   2. Imagination in literature.   3. Pragmatism in
literature.   4. Emerson, Ralph Waldo, 1803–1882—Influence—
Stevens.   5. James, William, 1842–1910.   I. Title.
PS3537.T4753Z674   1983   811'.52   83-40012
ISBN 0–87451–269–7

To Robert J. Bertholf

CONTENTS

4

PREFACE

he study that follows issues from a simple premise: examining the varieties of thinking displayed in the writing of Ralph Waldo Emerson and William James makes it possible to understand the significance of the sanctifying imagination in Wallace Stevens' poetry. Stevens' pivotal concepts regarding the function of language and metaphor, his portrayal of the subject-object dynamism, his adherence to the centrality of poetic vision and to the primacy of fiction over truth—all of these, when refracted through the prisms of Emerson's idealism and James's pragmatism, illuminate precise lines of influence in the emergence of the American self. Especially in his later poems, Stevens indicates that within an empirical universe, which he inherits from both Emerson and James, the imagination redeems itself continually by creative acts, transposing a drab existence within an "old chaos" into a secular and always sufficient paradise.

The specific cultural context from which the analysis evolves is clear enough. Emerson's stature in nineteenth-century American letters requires neither substantiation nor elaboration. He and the movement he sponsored have been studied and analyzed almost to a fault. What is most stimulating as an emphasis in current Emerson scholarship is not so much his impact on transcendentalism as a movement but rather his penetrative influence on contemporary writers and on contemporary thought. Thrilling to this truth, Emerson enthusiasts of today tend to forget that as recently as 1957, in his introduction to the Riverside edition of Emerson's collected essays, Stephen Whicher expressed a need to apologize for the fact that Emerson's "naive idealism no longer seems relevant" in a post-Darwinian era. By the mid-sixties, however, the contours of Emersonian influence on this century were surfacing more vividly. Hyatt Waggoner reverses Whicher's tentative stance when he adopts as the central thesis of his ambitious tome on American poets the contention that "Emerson is the central figure in American poetry, essential both as spokesman and as catalyst, not only the founder of the chief 'line' in our poetry but essential for an understanding of those poets not numbered among his poetic sons." Scholarship through the seventies and into the eighties corroborates and extends Waggoner's premise. If Whicher said of Emerson that "relatively few readers now find him a source of faith," Harold Bloom finds that Emerson's "truest achievement was to invent the American religion." For Bloom as well as for countless others, "the lengthened shadow of our American culture is Emerson's."

If general interest in Emerson is not particularly surprising, his specific relationship to William James and to the philosophy of pragmatism certainly is. Scholarly reappraisals of James and the provocative reconsideration of pragmatism as a vital contemporary philosophy have increased to a point where the renewed interest now constitutes what can only be termed a revival. The renascence centers in Richard Rorty, whose study clarifies in depth why Emerson and James should be linked. In *Consequences of Pragmatism*, Rorty stipulates that the opposition that crystallized in the nineteenth century between the transcendental philosophy and the empirical philosophy centered in the discussion of whether natural science contained all the Truth that could be found (positivism) or whether there was Truth beyond science (Platonism). Rorty argues convincingly that pragmatism resolves the contention insofar as it "cuts across this transcendental/empirical distinction by questioning the common presupposition that there is an invidious distinction to be drawn between kinds of truth." By lower casing "truth" and "philosophy," pragmatism pushes us into a "post-Philosophical culture." Removing the "halo" from truth, science, knowledge, and reality, William James enacts the replacement of romanticism by pragmatism.

The thrust of Rorty's argument, oversimplified here, specifies a strong theoretical base for the peculiar synthesis of Emerson's idealism and James's practicality. More pointedly, it provides a context for an extensive consideration of the telling impact of Emerson and James on Wallace Stevens, a confluence of imaginations that this book examines in detail.

The milieu established from which this study issues, an additional point should be made. Recent trends in literary aesthetics require that a prospective critic be acutely conscious of the tradition out of which he writes. To a growing number of theorists, principles of language and meaning adhered to for centuries are now open to serious challenge. That language communicates meaning, for instance, that it approximates feeling, or that it otherwise renders human experience into an intelligible form are no longer among the axioms a critic can presume. In his essay titled "How to Do Things with Texts," M. H. Abrams, announcing that the age of criticism is dead, regrets that the corpse has been replaced by the age of reading. In Abrams' glum portrayal, within the new age the human author is diminished to insignificance, man is "reduced to an illusion engendered by the play of language," and the human reader, "a wraith of his old self," becomes merely a "part of a systematic dehumanizing of all aspects of the traditional view about how a work of literature comes into being, what it is, how it is read, and what it means." Thus "humanistic" criticism, succumbing to the influence of such controversial and penetrating theorists as Jacques Derrida and Michel Foucault, deliquesces to textualism and structuralism. Aristotelian principles, in other words, become obsolete. Abrams even provides an "apocalyptic glimpse" into a new era in which artists and critics alike will inhabit a "totally textual universe whose reading is a mode of intertextuality whereby a subject-vortex engages with an object-abyss in infinite regressions of deferred significations."

Implicit in the study that follows is a rejection of this Orwellian specter looming within the new poetics. The exhortations of recent Stevens theorists such as Harold Bloom to grant "a priority to figurative language over meaning" or to "self over language" have been rejected in favor of the "humanistic" posture, which

presumes that a reader's task consists of an attempt to interpolate
an artist's intention within the context of linguistic norms, fluid
as they may be, shared by reader and author both. My intent
throughout this examination is to delineate what Stevens meant
to say in his poetry, not what the poems mean as "texts" distinct
from their author, and not what the reader "creates" them to
mean. Interestingly, when Stevens himself becomes critic to his
own poems, as he frequently does throughout his letters, he uses
such imperative clauses as "this poem consists of, . . ." or "here
is the right paraphrase," or "this . . . is intelligible language." In
so doing, it seems to me he acknowledges adherence to a shared
system of linguistic regularities from which he presumes his poems
to issue and from which he presumes a critic will approach them.

A synoptic review of the ensuing chapters may be helpful.
Chapter 1 divides the congruence of attitudes shared by Emerson,
James, and Stevens into four controlling categories and examines
each separately. Chapter 2 examines Stevens' poems up to "Notes
Toward a Supreme Fiction" from the point of view of Stevens'
early discovery that, in the tradition of Emerson's scholar, he
must take a central position in a world that is both pragmatic
and pluralistic. Chapter 3 considers the poems of *Transport to
Summer*, in which Stevens, like Emerson and James before him,
absorbs man-generated evil into his aesthetic, which enables him
in "Credences of Summer" to begin redeeming nature through
the medium of his own visions. Chapter 4 traces Stevens' efforts
as an aging man to evolve a rhetorical method through which he
could transform the flux of reality into language without sculpturally fixing it. In "The Auroras of Autumn" and "An Ordinary
Evening in New Haven," Stevens discovers an aesthetic counterpart to James's procedureless philosophical method and surpasses
the performance of Emerson's generative imagination. Chapter 5
considers Stevens' final achievement. In "The Rock," Stevens
culminates his lifelong assertion of the sacred foundation of empirical living and fulfills both Emerson's notion of the universe
as a wondrous visionary place and James's belief in the power of
man's mind to engender truth upon reality.

The forces that combine to produce a book are always awesome, and, like so much of reality that is especially significant, they transcend the power of language to account for them. Yet I shall try.

My deepest scholarly debt is to Robert J. Bertholf, whose brilliant critical eye perceived the scope of the subject and insured, from "naked Alpha" to "hierophant Omega," that I did not waver from it. His influence provides a vital key to whatever may be worthwhile in this study.

I am indebted for the free time needed to research and write the manuscript to the unparalleled generosity of Mr. John Wasmer. Opting to become a benefactor to scholarship is at best a risky venture; with this book as testimony to my appreciation, I extend once again to Mr. Wasmer a tactile thank-you with plenty of heart behind it.

I am grateful to Alfred A. Knopf, Inc., for permission to quote from the following copyrighted editions: *The Collected Poems of Wallace Stevens* (1954); *Opus Posthumous*, edited by Samuel French Morse (1957); *The Necessary Angel: Essays on Reality and the Imagination* (1951); and *Letters of Wallace Stevens*, edited by Holly Stevens (1966).

Thanks to my son, Michael, my daughter, Lisa, and my entire family from the smallest circle outward for modeling patience, support, and understanding throughout the project.

Finally, my deepest personal debt is to Rebecca Bode La Guardia. In circumstances most trying and extraordinary, she braved the scholar's gloom, selflessly stored the scars, and managed single-handedly, by her warm presence and wise pressuring, to transform a goal into an achievement. As she follows the process of her life, I wish for her always to cherish the half of this that is hers.

LIST OF ABBREVIATIONS

References to the following books by Ralph Waldo Emerson have been included in the text:

CWE *The Complete Works of Ralph Waldo Emerson.* 12 vols. Concord edition. Boston: Houghton, Mifflin, 1904.

LE   *The Letters of Ralph Waldo Emerson.* 6 vols. Ed. Ralph L. Rusk. New York: Columbia University Press, 1939.

EJ   *The Journals and Miscellaneous Notebooks of Ralph Waldo Emerson.* 16 vols. Ed. William Gilman. Cambridge: The Belknap Press of Harvard University Press, 1960.

References to the following books by William James have been included in the text. The original publication dates of James's works are given in parentheses. Unless otherwise indicated, page references in the text are to *The Writings of William James: A Comprehensive Edition,* ed. John J. McDermott (Chicago: University of Chicago Press, 1977).

CER *Collected Essays and Reviews.* New York: Longmans, Green, 1920. (1920)

ERE *Essays in Radical Empiricism.* New York: Longmans, Green, 1938. (1912)

LWJ *The Letters of William James.* 2 vols. Ed. Henry James, Jr. Boston: Atlantic Monthly Press, 1920.

MT   *The Meaning of Truth.* New York: Longmans, Green, 1932. (1909)

PP   *The Principles of Psychology.* New York: Henry Holt, 1927. (1890)

PR   *Pragmatism: A New Name for Some Old Ways of Thinking.* New York: Longmans, Green, 1947. (1907)

PU   *A Pluralistic Universe.* New York: Longmans, Green, 1932. (1909)

SPP   *Some Problems of Philosophy.* New York: Longmans, Green, 1948. (1911)

TT   *Talks to Teachers on Psychology: And to Students on Some of Life's Ideals.* New York: Henry Holt, 1912. (1897)

VRE   *The Varieties of Religious Experience.* New York: Longmans, Green, 1928. (1902)

WB   *The Will to Believe and Other Essays in Popular Philosophy.* New York: Henry Holt, 1912. (1897)

References to the following books by Wallace Stevens have been included in the text:

CP   *The Collected Poems of Wallace Stevens.* New York: Alfred A. Knopf, 1954.

LWS   *Letters of Wallace Stevens.* Ed. Holly Stevens. New York: Alfred A. Knopf, 1966.

NA   *The Necessary Angel: Essays on Reality and the Imagination.* New York: Vintage Books, 1951.

OP   *Opus Posthumous.* Ed. Samuel French Morse. New York: Alfred A. Knopf, 1957.

ADVANCE ON CHAOS

1 ADVANCE ON CHAOS
AND THE DARK

Framing the Argument

alph Waldo Emerson, William James, and Wallace Stevens create dynamic fictive theologies. Emerson's quarrel with the Unitarian church forced him to develop a philosophy based on the principle that "the one thing in the world, of value, is the active soul" (CWE 90).[1] William James, rejecting the strict procedures of Cartesian philosophy, discovers that "not in maxims . . . but in accumulated *acts* of thought lies salvation" (LWJ 147-48). And Wallace Stevens, in the tradition of his predecessors, boldly sidesteps the nihilism of the twentieth century by creating "the poem of the act of the mind" (CP 240). In each case, action, especially creative acts of thought, overcomes the loss of order and sustains man in his ambiguous and precarious position in the world. By acts of mind, each writer proposes that man submit himself to the compelling necessity of original perception.

The attitudes shared by James, Emerson, and Stevens divide into four distinct categories. First, each subscribes to a world in process, in which truth is a component not of idée fixe but of how the mind responds to reality's flux. Since nature enacts the forward process of change, man must concern himself not with absolute ideas of his own reality but with the particulars of his immediate world. Second, Emerson, James, and Stevens share a belief that the mind shapes the view of the reality it perceives, a premise that culminates in Wallace Stevens' concept of fictions. In the process of engendering truth upon reality, the mind must first release what it perceives from the sterility of old conceptions, which, for Stevens, evolves into a procedure of decreation. Third, all three writers project man at the center of his world. That man animates the processive world through his role in a nonteleological universe should be a factor not of depression or despair, but of freedom. Fourth, each denies the traditional concept of a dualism existing between subject and object, affirming instead that concept and percept interpenetrate. As the medium of communication, language achieves paramount significance in the subject-object dynamism. For Stevens, words, fictions themselves, embody the fictions by which man sustains himself.

These, then, are the considerations that will be examined. Wallace Stevens is a poet of the demythologized modern era whose lines to Emerson, the essayist of idealism, and James, the philosopher of practicality, define a provocative joining of forces that fulfills the earlier conception of the imagination as an agency of order. Examining the varieties of imagination displayed in the writing of Emerson and James makes it possible to understand the sanctifying imagination in Stevens' later poetry.

While several articles have been written on James and Emerson, and a few on James and Stevens or Emerson and Stevens, no extensive study of Stevens has examined the interrelationship of all three. As far back as 1929, Frederic Carpenter noticed the Emerson-James link by demonstrating that James was the "central figure of what should be called neo-transcendentalism in New England."[2] In 1946, inverting the premise, Eduard Lindeman affirmed Emerson's "pragmatic mood."[3] Practically every study of Stevens mentions Emerson, usually in passing, and several critics have noticed that Stevens implicitly follows James, yet neither strand has been fully traced and explained. Margaret Peterson christens James the philosophical father of *Harmonium*, but her contention that the later poetry veers away from James toward increasing aestheticism overlooks crucial aspects basic to pragmatism as well as to the later Stevens.[4] Calling Stevens a "radical transcendentalist," James Mulqueen hints at the collision of Emerson-James influence in Stevens but concentrates instead on the impact on Stevens of George Santayana.[5] In *Stevens' Poetry of Thought,* Frank Doggett notices several aspects of James's influence on Stevens. For instance, he suggests Stevens' familiarity with James's discussion in "The One and the Many" of the various kinds of continuity that bind the world together and hints that James's concept of truth may have influenced several of the poems. Yet his comments are brief and contextual.[6] Harold Bloom in his book on Stevens establishes a direct continuity in the poetic stances of Emerson and Stevens but concedes that Stevens learned most of Emerson's philosophy from Whitman.[7]

When Stevens proclaims in "Sunday Morning" that "We live in an old chaos of the sun," (CP 70)—one of a series of pronouncements by which he popularized for himself the title of Connoisseur of Chaos—he established a major common denominator between himself, James, and Emerson, namely, belief in a reality that has as its single fixity constant change, a reality based in process and multiplicity. In his copy of Emerson's essays, William James marked as "the motto for my book"[8] the passage in "Self-Reliance" where Emerson exults that "we are now men . . . not minors and invalids in a protected corner, not cowards fleeing before a revolution, but guides, redeemers and benefactors, obeying the Almighty effort and advancing on Chaos and the Dark" (CWE II 47). The fact of this "calculated chaos," as Stevens labels it in "Repetitions of a Young Captain" (CP 307), extends sufficient cause to Emerson for man to cease his dependence on archaic laws and forms and to return to the legitimacy of reliance upon his own perception. For William James, the reality of chaos becomes the structural base for the philosophy of pragmatism founded on the principles of a radical empiricism. For Stevens, the notion of the orderless flux of reality releases the imagination from adherence to the encrustations of old mythologies and sterile metaphors and permits fresh, creative utterance in a world "Where the voice that is great within us rises up, / As we stand gazing at the rounded moon" (CP 138).

The importance of a plastic world in Emerson stems not simply from the vestiges of a philosophy based on "man thinking" but from his concept of history as well. "There is no history. There is only biography," he writes in his journal; "the attempt to perpetuate, to fix a thought or principle, fails continually . . . your action is good only whilst it is alive,—whilst it is in you" (EJ VII 202). Relinquishing history from among the playthings of thinking man produces the "unsponsored, free" conditions of Stevens' world, wherein the inhabitants witness a fluxional reality, which in the multiplicity of its forms operates free of religious framework, social stratification, or historical categories. Morse Peckham theorizes that Emerson's rejection of history arises out of the comforting self-images that history offers to man. The self-reliant man, says Peckham, must "have the courage to doubt [his] comforting self-image."[9] Certainly Emerson's qualification of history anticipates Stevens' parallel dismissal of the old ideas of order ("exit the whole / Shebang. Exeunt Omnes." CP 37), and by deemphasizing the past, both writers plant themselves squarely before the spectacle of the "thousand-eyed present." The emphasis of the self as one perceived in the world reverts to the self as perceiver of the world, an inversion of man from the fringes of history to the crest of action. For the active man, as Emerson indicates, "history no longer shall be a dull book. It shall walk incarnate in every just and wise man" (CWE II 38). In "The Latest Freed Man," Stevens portrays a self who, because he is "Tired of the old descriptions of the world" (CP 204), rejects history and becomes an active man, "a man without a doctrine" perceiving his world as he had never before witnessed it.

Of course, as this discussion will later indicate, the nature of Emerson's idealism takes him beyond the interest in transience and phenomena for their own sake that typifies the theories of Stevens and James. What is significant in Emerson's case is that the given of his idealism did not prevent him from paying close attention to particulars and to change. Emerson never leaves the extent of the plasticity in the world in doubt. "Thin or solid, everything is in flight," he avers; "first innuendoes, then broad hints, then smart taps are given, suggesting that nothing stands still in Nature but death; that the creation is on wheels, in transit, always passing into something else" (CWE VIII 3–4). Such images of motion characterize his expression and illuminate his discovery in "Circles" of the underlying principle of a world in process: "every ultimate fact is only the first of a new series" (CWE II 304). Conformity and consistency, as emanations of commitment to history, stifle the free movement of the active mind to such a degree that Emerson posits madness as the condition of those who, through a fanaticism for fixity and order, deceive themselves by refusing to face the fundamental truth of nature that "nothing solid is secure: everything tilts and rocks" (CWE I 193). "We can never surprise nature in a corner," he theorizes,

never find the end of a thread. . . . The wholeness we admire in the order of the world is the result of infinite distribution. . . . Its permanence is a perpetual inchoation. . . . If anything could stand still, it would be crushed and dissipated by the torrent it resisted, and if it were a mind, would be crazed; as insane persons are those who hold fast to one thought and do not flow with the course of nature." (CWE I 199)

Static adherence to fixity and to stale historical contexts prompts Stevens in "Academic Discourse in Havana" to parody life as an "old casino in a park" (CP 142) where ancient, decaying structures fail to sustain man's creative energy. He attacks the politicians who "ordained / Imagination as the fateful sin" and fashioned an indolent existence for the masses amounting to nothing more than "a peanut parody / For peanut people" (CP 143). Like Emerson, Stevens wishes to purge the old structures—destroy them by imaginative acts—so that history cannot inhibit the mind's perception of "the gorgeous wheel" (CP 121) of reality that follows the paths of the imagination's flux. In his essay "Imagination as Value," Stevens mentions three specific enemies that threaten to overpower the imagination: logical positivism, Freudianism, and Communism. These represent major obstacles to the imagination in the modern world. In order to remain, as Stevens calls it, "one of the great human powers" (NA 138), the imagination must reject them and must avoid becoming locked into any other rigid systems of thought and action.

The fundamental difference between the fluxional world of Emerson and that of Stevens centers in Emerson's belief that "perpetual inchoation" flows from an "Eternal Cause" and advances toward unification: "All multiplicity rushes to be resolved into unity" (CWE VIII 7); "though abyss open under abyss, and opinion displace opinion, all are at last contained in the Eternal Cause" (CWE IV 186). The Unitarian base and the latent Puritan context out of which Emerson wrote contribute to these premises, even as the contexts of agnosticism and atheism in the twentieth century contribute to the premises of Stevens' writings. Though Stevens rejects the notion of absolute unity as part of the old romance that belongs on the dump, he transposes Emerson's notion of eternal cause into a figure for the imagination itself. In the *Adagia*, he states that "God is a symbol for something that can as well take other forms, as, for example, the form of high poetry" (OP 167); and in the late poem "Final Soliloquy of the Interior Paramour," he arrives at a clearer reconciliation of the two: "We say that God and the imagination are one" (CP 524). Even without identifying it to the imagination, Emerson's concept of eternal cause provides no artifice of security to his readers since, as he establishes in "The Over-Soul" and elsewhere, "the faith that stands on authority is not faith. The reliance on authority measures the decline of religion, the withdrawal of the soul" (CWE II 295). Although the particulars of his belief might have prevented him from agreeing with Stevens' dictum that "if nothing was the truth, then all / Things were the truth, the world itself was the truth" (CP 242), Emerson's categories are not at all restrictive: "The way of life is wonderful; it is by abandonment" (CWE II 321–22). The affirmation of divinity in a world of perpetual flux embodied for Emerson a challenge to his age to participate in divinity by more actively confronting the festival of life that reflected it. In the godless twentieth century, Stevens challenges his contemporaries to confront precisely the same festival, substituting for the divine the spirit of the holy that they generate in themselves by individual acts of the imagination's perception.

Commitment to a fluid universe is a vital characteristic in the attitudes of both men. Emerson's assertion that "there is no end in nature, but every end is a beginning" (CWE II 301) becomes Stevens' contention that the imagination "is always at the end of an era. What happens is that it is always attaching itself to a new reality" (NA 22). The confluence of theories and even phrases in the two writers specifies coincidence of imaginative visions.

William James, in the essays delineating his philosophy of pragmatism and the pluralistic nature of the universe, subscribes wholeheartedly to the same idea of a fluid reality. As John Mc-Dermott indicates, James was among the first—"if not the first"— to use the term "process" to describe the workings of consciousness in a fluxional world.[10] Echoing Emerson's phrase that "everything tilts and rocks," James realizes life as "something always off its balance, something in transition, something that shoots out of a darkness through a dawn into a brightness that we know to be the dawn fulfilled" (CER 158). Confronting the tragic predicament of having to choose between human experience as logical or as fundamentally irrational, almost triumphantly James "fairly, squarely and irrevocably" gives up the logic: "Reality, life, experience, concreteness, immediacy, use what word you will, exceeds our logic, overflows and surrounds it. . . . I myself find no good warrant for even suspecting the existence of any reality of a higher denomination than that distributed and strung-along and flowing sort of reality which we finite beings swim in" (PU 557–558). More cognitive and analytical than Emerson or Stevens, James defines a "melioristic universe" whose destiny "hangs on an if," which is to say that "the world being as yet unfinished, its total character can be expressed only by *hypothetical* and not by *categorical* propositions" (SPP 739). One could readily conjecture Stevens' canon of poetry to be an extension of the if-dependency of the universe; the tentative titles he gives many of his poems—"Notes Toward . . . ," "Nuances of . . . ," "Like Decorations . . . ," "Variations on . . . ," "Prelude to Objects . . . ," and so on,—specify a lasting inclination on Stevens' part toward hypothetical gesturing rather than categorical determinations about a world-in-process.

The issues of absolute unity and eternal cause absorbed by Emerson dissolve in James's insistence that "nothing outside of the flux secures the issue of it" (PR 457). Conceding that "the unity of the world is on the whole undergoing increase" (ERE 213–14), he refuses to concede in turn that absolute unity will be experienced: "The generalized conclusion is that . . . parts of experience hold together from next to next by relations that are themselves parts of experience. The directly apprehended universe needs, in short, no extraneous trans-empirical connective support, but possesses in its own right a concatenated or continuous structure" (MT 136). For James, Emerson's "thousand-eyed present" and Stevens' "The present close, the present realized" (CP 238) become the "instant field of the present" wherein experience in its "pure" state occurs (ERE 208). But each present moment proliferates by transition into the next moment and so on continually, so that "life is in the transitions as much as in the terms connected" (ERE 212). James concludes that in a sense "literally no such object as the present moment except as an unreal postulate of abstract thought" exists (PU 294). Throughout Stevens' poetry appear variations on James's concept of the flux of time. In "Thirteen Ways of Looking at a Blackbird" (CP 92), the thrust of the present moment exerts energy on the imagination; the poem expands through thirteen "instant fields of the present" during which the imagination creates from the mutations it perceives. Whether in open- or closed-form poems, Stevens postulates throughout his work a Jamesian time-stream in which "the *passing* moment is the only thing that ever concretely was or is or shall be" (CER 158). When Stevens conjectures in "An Ordinary Evening in New Haven" that "Among time's images, there is not one / Of this present" (CP 476), he means that the venerable masks of the old images can never be used to describe fresh moments because "The oldest-newest day is the newest alone" (CP 476). Each "newest" day becomes part of a stream of yesterdays. In the flow of time, the newest day must be described in newest images so that aspects essential to it are not distorted by stale images. By extension, this explains why the old images from all the old moments belong on his renowned "dump." A world-in-process is ruthless in its relinquishing of outmoded forms because "life is the elimination of what is dead" (OP 169).

The shift of attention away from wholeness and absolutes corresponds to a shift toward concentration on particulars, the core factor in James's pluralistic philosophy as well as the starting point in Stevens' poetic system. Whereas rationalism is "monistic," starts with universals and attends to the unity of things, James's empiricism "starts from the parts, and makes of the whole a collection—is not averse therefore to calling itself pluralistic" (PR 365). Calling it a "mosaic philosophy" and a "philosophy of plural facts," James notes that empiricism stresses the part, the element, making the whole or the all of secondary consideration:

the pluralistic view which I prefer to adopt is willing to believe that there may ultimately never be an all-form at all, that the substance of reality may never get totally collected . . . and that a distributive form of reality, the *each*-form, is logically as acceptable and empirically as probable as the all-form commonly acquiesced in. (PU 494)

James envisions a world of "innumerable little hangings together" wherein nothing (thus the radical aspect of his empiricism) may be either admitted or excluded unless experienced directly. Whatever is perceived in the whole must first have been perceived in the parts because "the only material we have at our disposal for making a picture of the whole world is supplied by the various portions of that world" (PU 484).

James's "portions of that world," by a minor vocabulary adjustment, becomes the title of Stevens' third book of poems, *Parts of a World*, in which the imagination responds, in poem after poem, to reality in its sundry parts—a glass of water, two pears, a dry loaf, an old horn, and so forth. With James, Stevens recognizes that the imagination "loses vitality as it ceases to adhere to what is real" (NA 6) and that "reality is things as they are" (NA

25). Writing out of a world in which the old social, religious, and political hierarchies have crumbled and in which the consequent dependence on "all-form" is less and less possible, of necessity Stevens subscribes to a universe relieved of wholeness except that which he furnishes by separate acts of the imagination. His collection of poems represents his version of a world of "innumerable little hangings together," parts of a world in which the poet must establish anew a relationship to the elementary things of life. In "The Man on the Dump," the dump is "full / Of images" because it overflows with the descriptions by which the old poets described the parts of their world, and which now have no poetic authenticity.

> So the sun,
> And so the moon, both come, and the janitor's poems
> Of every day, the wrapper on the can of pears,
> The cat in the paper-bag, the corset, the box
> From Esthonia: the tiger chest, for tea.
>
> (CP 201)

In "Landscape With Boat," Stevens creates a rhapsody to parts as the essence of a pluralistic world:

> He never supposed
> That he might be truth, himself, or part of it,
> That the things that he rejected might be part
> And the irregular turquoise, part, the perceptible blue
> Grown denser, part, the eye so touched, so played
> Upon by clouds, the ear so magnified
> By thunder, parts, and all these things together,
> Parts, and more things, parts.
>
> (CP 242)

In such a system, chance, novelty, and surprise, as much as any concrete objects, become aspects of reality, and arguments involving the fine shadowings of philosophical premises pertain at all only if they affect in some practical way a factual situation. James illustrates:

It is astonishing to see how many philosophical disputes collapse into insignificance the moment you subject them to this simple test. There can be no difference which doesn't make a difference—no difference in abstract truth which does not express itself in a difference of concrete fact, and of conduct consequent upon the fact, imposed on somebody, somehow, somewhere, and somewhen. (CER 349)

The pragmatic test that James applies to abstract truth stipulates that the truth must express itself in a difference of concrete fact or it is meaningless. That is, if it does not affect the "parts" of a world, it cannot affect the whole.

The philosophy of pragmatism energizes existence by drawing man's attention out of theory back to the vibrant, physical world. Instead of assuming previous hypotheses, pragmatism demands new ones originating from renewed physical contact. A philosophy of facticity, it urges what Emerson urged in "Nature," that each man form an original relation to the universe by opening to himself the possibility of primary insights. Wallace Stevens constructs his philosophy of poetry on the same foundation. Realizing the sterility of dogma and the boredom of imitation, Stevens insists on turning to the world of primary fact stripped of the paraphernalia of history and man's traditions and reconstructing through creative acts of the mind a vital relationship to his world. He fulfills therefore not only Emerson's definition of the American scholar but James's description of pragmatism as well. The pragmatist, says James,

turns away from abstraction and insufficiency, from verbal solutions, from bad *a priori* reasons, from fixed principles, closed systems, and pretended absolutes and origins. He turns towards concreteness and adequacy, towards facts, towards action. . . . It means the open air and possibilities of nature, as against dogma, artificiality, and the pretence of finality in truth. (PR 379)

In Stevens' phrase, it means discovering the time when "Everything is shed" and "you see / As a man (not like an image of a man)" (CP 202) a reality that must be confronted without preconceptions in that moment where "one first heard of the truth . . . The the" (CP 203).

Emerson's philosophy of idealism adheres to a pluralistic uni-

verse of particulars also. He rejects the scholars who lose themselves in theories, become pedants, or fail to comprehend that
man must converse with a world of parts. He anticipates James's
"ever-not-quite" approach to reality by preferring the imperfect
over the perfect and by being satisfied not with Truth as rigid
structure, but with glimpses of truth rising out of flux. Illustrating
Stevens' concept that "we have been a little insane about the
truth," (NA 33) Emerson proclaims a faith interpreted through
facticity: "faith should blend with the light of rising and of setting suns, with the flying cloud, the singing bird, and the breath
of flowers" (CWE I 137)—in short, with the vibrancy of the
flowing world. In a journal entry, Emerson demonstrates what
happens when the intellect, at first bored by the stream of facts,
becomes suddenly stimulated:

Day creeps after day each full of facts—dull, strange, despised things
that we cannot enough despise. . . . And presently the aroused intellect finds gold & gems in one of these scorned facts, then finds that
the day of facts is a rock of diamonds . . . that on every fact of his
life he should rear a temple of wonder, joy, & praise. (EJ VII 29)

Not surprisingly, in a pluralistic philosophy based upon the
discovery of the possibilities of nature, the eye becomes the organ
of transference from dependence on the old to participation in
the new; as the mind's camera, the eye pans unrestrictedly the
process world and establishes the initial relation by which mind
and reality fuse. For James, Emerson, and Stevens alike, the death
of fixity is the mother of ripeness because it removes from the eye
the old mythologies and preconstructions and permits fresh vision
of the world's flow. When Stevens discovers that

> It was when I said,
> "There is no such thing as the truth,"
> That the grapes seemed fatter

(CP 203)

he acknowledges the importance to imagination of the release
from the structures of the past and affirms instead the discon-
nected particulars of a present world as the sole arena of luxury.

But appreciation of the present world requires first *seeing* it clearly. Reestablishment of an original relation to the universe begins in the eye as the "first circle" and medium of perception. Emerson's momentous statement, "I become a transparent eyeball; I am nothing; I see all" (CWE I 10) was converted by Stevens in "Asides on the Oboe" into "The central man, the human globe . . . the man of glass . . . the transparence of the place in which / He is" (CP 250–51). Similarly, in "Owl's Clover," using another image of Emerson's transparent eyeball, he describes the lord of memory as "A wandering orb upon a path grown clear" (OP 70). Stevens insists that "The world must be measured by eye" (CP 204), which recalls in turn the double emphasis James gives to the same conclusion: "Let me repeat once more that a man's vision is the great fact about him" (PU 489).

The fundamental similarities in the philosophies of Emerson and James as they relate to Stevens established, the important issue must yet be considered as to how a philosophy that eliminates all the old scaffolding of systematic belief from its basic tenets should become for its adherents a source not of despair but of consolation. The consolation and freedom that surface in Stevens' nonteleological universe relate him directly to Emerson and James since, in the case of each, the sources for hope arise from the premise that man must relinquish old truths and must make his own truth. With God removed from the top link in the great chain of being, the chain itself dissolves into individual links, becomes a pluralism where the perceiving self observes the parts from the center, the point from which Stevens abandons the advocates of a waste land and reconstructs in a mode of triumph a vibrant relation to his world. Yet the triumph evolves· from the fresh conception of truth that replaces the archaic notions.

In a system of process, truth depends not upon abstract fixity but on the interaction of mind and object, a notion that all three writers support and that anticipates Stevens' concept of "fictions." James illustrates that the truths of his present writing "the morrow may reduce . . . to 'opinion' " (ERE 208), while Emerson conceives "no truth so sublime but it may be trivial tomorrow in the light of new thoughts" (CWE II 320). When Stevens notices "one more truth, one more / Element in the immense disorder of truths" (CP 216), the disorder implies nothing pejorative, but rather admission that, as pragmatism teaches, truths evolve from facts that are a part of an experienceable reality in the process of everlasting mutation; truths then emerge from facts and add to facts as the facts in turn reveal new truths. Emerson exhorts a similar premise in his journal: "truth . . . must *live* every moment in the beginning, in the middle, & onward forever in every stage of statement" (EJ VII 232). The consolation for affirming truths as adhering to process rather than absolutes enables man to "bear the disappearance of things he was wont to reverence without losing his reverence" (CWE IV 186), says Emerson. Similarly consoled, Stevens can "Let be be finale of seem" (CP 64) without regret that the platitudes of "seem" have evaporated.

Although not to the extent of James or Stevens, Emerson noticed that truth vibrates indefinitely in the field set up between the mind and the flickering of parts within the mind's perception, that the mind contributes to the shaping of the reality it perceives. Slightly adjusting Heraclitus' famous maxim, Emerson avers that "a man never sees the same object twice" because "with his own enlargement the object acquires new aspects" (CWE I 214). More to the point, he asserts that "we . . . put our own interpretation on things" (CWE I 160), and that the problem of restoring an ugly world to beauty resides "in our own eye" (CWE I 73) since, when a man is out of phase with himself, the world unravels proportionately. He realizes in the essay "Experience" that "there is no end to illusion" and that "life is a train of moods like a string of beads, and as we pass through them they prove to be many-colored lenses which paint the world their own hue, and each shows only what lies in its focus" (CWE III 50). The passage concludes with the statement by which Emerson places himself dead-center in Stevens' fictive world: "We animate what we can, and we see only what we animate" (CWE III 50). With Stevens, Emerson locates the source of reality's vibrancy in the creative energy of imaginative acts. In the *Adagia*, Stevens rephrases Emerson's idea that "we see only what we animate": "Reality is not what it is. It consists of the many realities which it can be made into" (OP 178).

Animating what we can by acts of imagination, putting our own interpretation on things—little wonder that the loss of his "shaping power of imagination" so dejected Coleridge; the withdrawal of the old systems of order bequeaths to the imagination a heritage of awesome import, which, to be without, especially for the poet, might well be devastating. The possible no longer circumscribed by faith or in any way invested by spiritual categories, the mind must return to the core of a physical world and investigate for itself the lineaments of belief and of possibility. "The imagination is the power of the mind over the possibility of things," Stevens announces in "Imagination as Value"; "it is the source not of a certain single value but of as many values as reside in the possibilities of things" (NA 136). For the imagination to be the source of values, its primary function must be to invest what man perceives in the flux of particulars with an order or a truth that then may be altered by the endless profusion of new particulars. But the particulars within the flux consist already of the order and truth that past imaginative acts have discovered in them. These previous systems prevent accurate perception of the flux, so the imagination must eliminate the old ideas in order to discover new ones. Decreation must precede creation. The discoveries of truth or order emanating from this destruction-creation process depend upon the imagination as a powerful creative force. Since the imagination manifests itself in words that are but metaphors of the real world, but as close as we can get to it, the conclusion inevitably surfaces that the order and truth in the pluralistic universe can never by anything other than metaphorical. Words represent sounds that man devises to represent or take

the place of objects. Although the habit of language deceives man
into thinking that the sounds he uses for objects are the objects
themselves, in fact they are not. Words are always distinctly separate from the reality they describe. They are man's invention of
reality, fabrications so long used that they pass for the facts themselves. Emerson notices that "language is made up of images or
tropes, which now, in their secondary use, have long ceased to
remind us of their poetic origin" (CWE III 22). Since one thing
standing for another is the basis of metaphor, and since words stand
for objects, then all language is metaphorical. "Every word was
once a poem," Emerson writes; "every new relation is a new word"
(CWE III 18). (In the *Adagia*, Stevens writes: "A new meaning is the equivalent of a new word" [OP 159].) Man communicates not reality but metaphors of reality, sounds expressing the
influence of objects on the mind. The poet, then, in Emerson's
phrase, becomes "Namer or Language-maker"—one who "names
the thing because he sees it, or comes one step nearer to it than
any other" (CWE III 21–22). The poet's function indicates the
force of the imagination. The creative use of language involves
decreasing the semantic distance between reality and words, an
impossible goal, yet a logical thrust of man's realization that he
communicates an approximation of reality rather than reality itself.

In short, he communicates fictions. For Wallace Stevens as well
as for William James, the concept of fictions constitutes the basic
factor of their writings. In the *Adagia*, Stevens renders his clearest
pronouncement on the subject: "The final belief is to believe in a
fiction, which you know to be a fiction, there being nothing else.
The exquisite truth is to know that it is a fiction and that you
believe in it willingly" (OP 163). He repeats the concept in the
opening lines of "Asides on the Oboe," a poem that registers a
crucial turning point in the growth of his theory:

> The prologues are over. It is a question, now,
> Of final belief. So, say that final belief
> Must be in a fiction. It is time to choose.

(CP 250)

Here is a poet of the disenfranchised modern era choosing the position with which he had toyed repeatedly in "the prologues" of his early poetry: that final belief rests not in faith, God, or immortality, but in the fictions of the mind's creation, and that poetry, as the "supreme fiction," is simply a "response to the daily necessity of getting the world right" (OP 176). For Stevens, fictions are proposals that temporarily satisfy the imagination's hunger for belief but are not taken as absolute truths. "In the long run," he tells us, "truth does not matter" (OP 180). The "exquisite truth" of knowing all to be a fiction and willingly subscribing to that knowledge obviates for Stevens the duality of the mind's "blessed rage for order" in an orderless world, for it substitutes the mind's versions of order to quench the rage temporarily. Poetry thus "creates a fictitious existence on an exquisite plane" (OP 180) by approximating reality through the imagination's vision of it. The poet must not submit to the temptation of rendering absolute truth from his approximations for he knows that reality is not what it is but what he makes it, that it "consists of the many realities which it can be made into" (OP 178).

Stevens' concept of fictions derives from William James. Truth for James arises out of the process of existence attaching itself to previous truth and modifying it accordingly. The core of his thesis explains that "truth *happens* to an idea. It *becomes* true, is *made* true by events. Its verity *is* in fact an event, a process" (PR 430). Yet James proceeds even more dramatically than this toward a hypothesis of fictions. He recognizes that in the flux of things, the individual tries to satisfy his desire for novelty by assimilating new experiences and old beliefs. Thus, "when old truth grows . . . by new truth's addition, it is for subjective reasons" (PR 384), which establishes a humanistic basis for truth. Since he believes that "without selective interest, experience is an utter chaos" (PP xxxviii), James posits a situation whereby each man, by means of the creative principle operating in both his cognitive and his active life, imbues with truth those parts of the flux that he selects. In short, he creates what is true of his world: "so from one thing to another, altho the stubborn fact remains that there *is* a sensible flux, what is *true of it* seems from first to last to be largely a matter of our own creation" (PR 455).

Creations of the mind, which James calls truths, as well might be called fictions. By affirming that the final belief is to believe in a fiction, Stevens aligns himself to the specific Jamesian premise that "mind *engenders* truth *upon* reality," for the fictions in which Stevens believes are the truths he engenders in poems by the act of the mind. James elaborates how acts of the mind re-model reality:

Mind *engenders* truth *upon* reality. . . . Our minds are not here simply to copy a reality that is already complete. They are here to complete it, to add to its importance by their own remodeling of it, to decant its contents over, so to speak, into a more significant shape. In point of fact, the *use* of most of our thinking is to help us to *change* the world.[11]

James recognized that the familiar notion of truth as the duplication by the mind of a given reality was not acceptable because "there is no simple test available for adjudicating offhand between the divers types of thought that claim to possess it" (PR 428). As a procedure of utility, the philosophy of pragmatism argues that if an unresolvable conflict exists concerning who possesses the truth, then the notion of truth itself must be over-hauled. James discards categorically the "great assumption of the intellectualists" that describes truth as "an inert static relation" that, once possessed, is the "end of the matter . . . you *know*; you have fulfilled your thinking destiny" (PR 430). He vilifies those philosophers who represent the universe as "a queer sort of petrified sphinx," positing truth as a monotonous solidity reminiscent of Stevens' many statues:

The truth: what a perfect idol of the rationalistic mind! I read in an old letter—from a gifted friend who died too young—these words: "In everything, in science, art, morals and religion, there *must* be one system that is right and *every* other wrong." How characteristic of the enthusiasm of a certain stage of youth! At twenty-one we rise to such a challenge and expect to find the system. It never occurs to most of us even later that the question "what is *the* truth?" is no real question (being irrelative to all conditions) and that the whole notion of *the* truth is an abstraction from the fact of truths in the plural, a mere useful summarizing phrase like *the* Latin Language or *the* Law. (PR 450)

Unleashed from precept and dogma, truth for William James partakes of the rich phenomena of the mind's daily experiences. Novelty and sensation, anathemas to the rationalist's conception of truth, become essential ingredients to the empiricist. New opinions count as "true" for James in proportion as they gratify an individual's "desire to assimilate the novel in his experience" (PR 384). Yet the process of assimilation depends finally upon feeling because "a conception is reckoned true by common sense when it can be made to lead to a sensation" (ERE 309). Since ideas are parts of experience, they are true only insofar as they assist in getting other parts of experience into satisfactory relation. Truth thus serves as a bridge, a "smoother-over of transitions" (PR 383) as the mind sifts through the phenomena it selects from the flux of reality. "Pragmatism gets her general notion of truth," James writes, "as something essentially bound up with the way in which one moment in our experience may lead us towards other moments which it will be worthwhile to have been led to" (PR 431–32).

Wallace Stevens expresses these "flicks" (CP 385) of worthwhile moments as poems, and the truth contained in them is "the more than rational distortion, / The fiction that results from feeling" (CP 406) when the imagination responds to the energy of reality's pressure and creates from the swarming continuum, through language, a proposal for order. As impermanent as James's truths, Stevens' fictions compensate for crumbled teleology by the vitality and freshness of their insight. They extend to the poet the excitement of perceiving the world in the context of its teeming process and of creating metaphors of those processes within the mind's own flux. In "Notes Toward a Supreme Fiction," Stevens isolates the source of the enjoyment of creating fictions:

> These things at least comprise
> An occupation, an exercise, a work,

A thing final in itself and, therefore, good:
One of the vast repetitions final in
Themselves and, therefore, good, the going round

And round and round, the merely going round,
Until merely going round is a final good.

(CP 405)

Since life is irrational, "poetry must be irrational" (OP 162), yet the fictions it creates are of the highest form since through poetry alone does the mind enact in fullest potential the ritual of creation.

Despite the similarities mentioned earlier, some differences between Emerson on the one hand and James and Stevens on the other become clear on this subject of fictions. Although Emerson subscribes to the moment of immediate insight as the source of any truth and believes we see only what we animate, he proposes not that the mind engenders truth but that it discovers it by acute witness to nature's spectacle. He extends to himself and his readers the consolation of a residual teleology, which it is the challenge of the scholar to locate by original insight. When the young mind goes to nature and "classification begins," Emerson delights in the tyranny of the mind's "unifying instinct," which "goes on tying things together, diminishing anomalies, discovering roots running under ground whereby contrary and remote things cohere and flower out from one stem." He concludes this passage from "The American Scholar" by asking: "But what is classification but the perceiving that these objects are not chaotic, and are not foreign, but have a law which is also a law of the human mind" (CWE I 85–86). Emerson's "unifying instinct" echoes Stevens' "blessed rage for order," but the point remains that, while for all three writers the unifying of contrary and remote things occurs through acts of the mind, for Emerson the unity exists whether the mind discovers it or not; for James and Stevens, it exists solely because the mind created it.

Emerson believes truth to exist in the design of the universe; Stevens, and in a different sense, James, in the release of a designing imagination. Consequently, the world looms more alien and tentative to James and Stevens, the chaos is more profound, and the need for the mind to create satisfactory fictions more urgent. In an early journal entry, Stevens admits "it would be much *nicer* to have things definite—both human and divine. One wants to be decent and to know the reason why. I think I'd enjoy being an executioner, or a Russian policeman" (LWS 86–87). Certainly these professions would permit him reliance on the fictions of others instead of needing to create his own perpetually. Similarly, James recognizes the peril that his philosophy of pragmatism pressures him into a dangerous and adventurous universe where "there should be real losses and real losers, and no total preservation of all that is" (PR 470); yet, like Stevens, he embraces these risks as aspects of the only philosophical system that he can accept: "while I freely admit that the pluralism and the restlessness are repugnant and irrational in a certain way, I find that every alternative to them is irrational in a deeper way" (WB 606).

The ramifications of subscribing to a fictive world indeed are awesome. In the preface to his book *Man's Rage for Chaos*, Morse Peckham argues that since the artist's approach to reality breaks up orientations that the drive for order establishes, artistic expression satisfies not the tyrannous appetite for order, as is customarily assumed, but rather an appetite for chaos. The tendency toward order in man prevents him, Peckham says, from approaching a new situation with an open mind because he brings to it predispositions formed from incidents previous and similar to it. By placing the archetype of an older situation comfortably over the new, man satisfies his appetite for order. But he smothers aspects of the situation that do not fulfill his expectations and by which he could grow. Thus does the rage for order disqualify him from an accurate perception of a new reality.[12]

On a grand scale, Peckham's theory applies to the notion of fictions in Stevens and James. Once having discovered the sterility of absolutes and the nonexistence of spiritual securities, Stevens recognizes that to support the old manifestations of people's rages for order, the old fictions, is to become stuck in the mud of superimposed archetypes and to hover on the periphery of reality, not at the center. The poet, for instance, in proportion as he borrows from old poetic forms and images to describe present facts, separates himself from the vitality of active perception. The challenge for the poet in a disenfranchised universe involves stripping from reality all vestiges of the old fictions, discarding the familiar images, and re-dressing reality each time he perceives it in a fresh language of new fictions. For this reason, Stevens infers that the imagination is most fertile when it seems to have no place to go and confronts reality in its most primitive form. In "Evening Without Angels," the poet experiences a vision of ecstasy *after* he has rejected seraphim, haloes, and other vestiges of Christianity and has realized that "Bare night is best. Bare earth is best. Bare, bare, / Except for our own houses" (CP 137–38). Only in this way can the modern poet write "The poem of the mind in the act of finding / What will suffice" (CP 239). Stevens recognizes that the mind did not always need to search and find, that it had only to repeat "what / Was in the script" (CP 239). But when "the theater . . . changed" and the gods disappeared, the imagination needed either to embrace sterile forms or to decreate the old world and return somehow to reality's essential core. By acts of mind he would engender new truths that he would know to be vital fictions closer to the heart of the flux than any of the old myths had ever permitted him to come.

Whether in Emerson's theories of idealism, James's philosophy of pragmatism, or Stevens' poetry of fictions, man as the creator of his own world commands vital significance. No longer the inheritor of design but the creator of it, man, for Stevens, unites himself intimately to reality's gorgeous wheel and shifts from the periphery of a spiritual world to the center of a godless but nevertheless holy world. Images of the center abound in the works of Emerson, James, and Stevens alike. Since the eye is the first circle, the self as perceiver occupies the circle's pivotal point, extending infinite radii outward to the horizons that the eye forms. "Rightly, poetry is organic," Emerson writes in the essay "Poetry and Imagination"; "we cannot know things by words and writing, but only by taking a central position in the universe and living in its forms"

(CWE VIII 42). In "The Uses of Great Men," he says that as "a man is a centre for nature, running out threads of relation through every thing . . . so every organ, function, acid, crystal, grain of dust, has its relation to the brain" (CWE IV 9). In "Self-Reliance," he writes that "a true man belongs to no other time or place, but is the centre of things" (CWE II 60), and in "The Poet" he emphasizes that the poet "is the sayer, the namer. . . . He is a sovereign, and stands on the centre" (CWE III 7). Finally, in "The Transcendentalist," Emerson clearly establishes that the perceiving mind of man is the necessary pivot in a process world:

> [The idealist's] thought—that is the universe. His experience inclines him to behold the procession of facts you call the world, as flowing perpetually outward from an invisible, unsounded centre in himself, centre alike of him and of them, and necessitating him to regard all things as having a subjective or relative existence, relative to that aforesaid Unknown Centre of him. (CWE I 334)

Harold Bloom has made an important attempt to synthesize the image of the central man in Emerson. He traces it through Whitman to Stevens and comes to this relevant conclusion: "Whatever the dangers of the Emersonian vision of the center, we have no choice but to seek the light of that vision, for it is the major example yet given us in America of what Stevens might have called the human making choice of a human self."[13] For Stevens, the "choice of a human self" constitutes a strong affirmation and implies rejection of all dependency on the divine self. Discussing the same three writers, Roy Harvey Pearce writes that "Stevens, like Emerson and Whitman before him, dared search for the ground on which the modern American self might base its sense of its own identity and so carry out its historical mission."[14]

For Emerson, man's position at the center of his cosmos illustrates the exchange of roles evolving from the shift of living in the dry bones of the past to living in an original relation to the universe. Many have illustrated that Walt Whitman reflects the fullest example of this shift, expressing in his songs of self the vitality of man's condition when he positions himself in the flux of existence and, by launching "filament, filament, filament," construes reality from the axis of his own being outward. Yet the auspicious antithesis of creating the world anew requires a concomitant decreation whereby the mind of the poet relinquishes from its categories the clutter of old metaphor, outmoded mythologies and other such conformities and consistencies of little minds. Both Emerson and Wallace Stevens adopt such procedures of decreation in their respective worlds; to achieve a closer relation to the universe, the central man in Emerson—his "scholar" as representative man (which for Stevens has its variants in the rabbi, the major man, and the hero)—must strip away the old forms in order to perceive the value of life in the present. "The new man," says Emerson, "must feel that he is new, and has not come into the world mortgaged to the opinions and usages of Europe, and Asia, and Egypt" (CWE I 159). Only thus can man achieve what he calls in "The Poet" the "true nectar," which derives from the "ravishment of the intellect by coming nearer to the fact" (CWE III 28).

For Stevens, the ravishment of coming nearer to the fact (a way of approaching the center) demands of poetry that it be a destructive force. In "Poetry Is a Destructive Force," poetry becomes a dog, bear, ox, and lion—images of power that, unleashed, "can kill a man" (CP 193). In "Man and Bottle," Stevens explains that the mind must be "more than the man"; it must be

> A man with the fury of a race of men,
> A light at the centre of many lights.
> A man at the centre of men.
>
> (CP 239)

The position of the center, more elusive for Stevens than for Emerson, requires for its attainment a furious effort on the part of the mind acting through poems to destroy the old structures:

> The poem lashes more fiercely than the wind,
> As the mind, to find what will suffice, destroys
> Romantic tenements of rose and ice.
>
> (CP 239)

Stevens incarnates the American scholar as the "latest freed man," or major man, or hero—one who, "Tired of the old descriptions of the world" (CP 204), confronts reality "Like a man without a doctrine," without prescription or predisposition. He is one able to reach back to a primitive state, what Stevens calls elsewhere the state of the "ignorant man," who may be the one alone who "Has any chance to mate his life with life" (CP 222). Being without a doctrine renders this man central and powerful; it is "to have the ant of the self changed to an ox" (CP 205). From the pigmy-ant on the edge of things, the shift to center by acts of decreation transforms individuals into major men:

> They make
> The giants that each one of them becomes
> In a calculated chaos.
>
> (CP 307)

The pluralistic world perceived from a central position undergoes a transformation similar to that of the latest freed man as, in the light of the shaping imagination, it is released from petrifaction and sterility and floats like one of Stevens' animated statues in a vibrant reality.

By fostering man's reacquaintance to himself, Emerson kindled the release of the American imagination and established the base by which the self could sustain itself through periods of violent disruption. He anticipated not so much the void of James's and Stevens' world, but the heroic and creative temperament for living in it. "If there is any period one would desire to be born in," he wrote in "The American Scholar," "is it not the age of Revolution; when the old and the new stand side by side and admit of being compared; when the energies of all men are searched by fear and hope" (CWE I 110).

The idealism of Stevens operating in the waste land of the twentieth century and the philosophy of pragmatism that James developed out of a decision not to commit suicide can be understood better by recognizing the impetus Emerson gave to man to situate himself at the center and to partake of heroism. "I will not say man is to man a wolf," he wrote in his journal in 1837; "but man should be to man a hero" (EJ V 421).

The drift of common man to the position of hero extends logically from the nature of the pluralistic and processive world that Emerson, James, and Stevens all support. Insofar as man is the sole arbiter of the world in which he lives, he assumes the inevitable and sometimes unwelcome role—if he wishes to have significance at all—of becoming hero to himself and to his fellows. The closer he permits himself to come to the center of his cosmos—that is, the more he decreates his world, becomes self-reliant, and animates otherwise inert things—the more heroic he becomes, since, in effect, he defeats his chaos by confronting it squarely and creates himself anew with each act of the mind. The reasons, then, why the fact of a nonteleological universe is a source not of dejection and despair for Stevens and James but of freedom and hope, become clearer. The options for man upon facing the possibility of the death of the gods and of design are either to make the leap of faith T. S. Eliot made and return to the security of the Christian redemptive myth, or to face the reality of living in a world without traditional spiritual myths. Although acceptance of the latter option produces despair for many, for James and Stevens the void that survives the death of the gods contains the same pluralistic base it contained before their demise. Through an ironic reversal of the Christian myth, the fall of the gods becomes man's *felix culpa,* by which he experiences in a kind of baptismal renewal immersion into the dynamic flow. He redeems himself into an earthly "paradise," no less sacred than the one he lost, by the power of his own visions. The very tentativeness of his position renders more authentic the celebration of his imagination's power.

In a processive world, the position of the center emerges fleetingly. Although Stevens expresses in one poem that

> It would be enough
> If we were ever, just once, at the middle, fixed
> In This Beautiful World of Ours and not as now,
> Helplessly at the edge   (CP 430)

he realizes that "The essential poem at the centre of things" comes in momentary and fleeting visions: "It is and it / Is not and, therefore, is" (CP 440). The vision of the center comes and goes, and because it does that, it is authentic. If the vision remained, it would be fixed; the elusiveness defines a controlling aspect of its centrality. Stevens explains that "clairvoyant men" compose central poems and "One poem proves another" (CP 441) until the "used-to earth" loses the old uses and vibrates anew; the accumulation of individual poems becomes part of the central poem of the world and the clairvoyant men—or poets— form the composite of the major man "At the center on the horizon, concentrum, grave / And prodigious person, patron of origins" (CP 443). Surely, Stevens' concept of the major man as "A giant on the horizon, given arms" (CP 443) advances the image Emerson foresaw for the man who in the creative powers of his mind could recreate reality from his own animation. Yet the tentativeness of the central position restates James as well, who, in the pluralistic universe, seeks a center that, as quickly as it can be achieved, dissolves:

I feel that there is a centre in truth's forest where I have never been: to track it out and get there is the secret spring of all my poor life's philosophic efforts; at moments I almost strike into the final valley, there is a gleam of the end, a sense of certainty, but always there comes still another ridge, so my blazes merely circle towards the true direction; and although now, if ever, would be the fit occasion, yet I cannot take you to the wondrous hidden spot to-day. To-morrow it must be, or to-morrow, or to-morrow, and pretty surely death will overtake me ere the promise is fulfilled. (CER 347)

This statement contains in miniature a characterization of the whole of Stevens' poetry. If James's figures of the flickering center are not a direct source for Stevens' figures of center and edge, which they very well could be, they portray at least a brilliant example of the psychic affinity between the two writers. Creating from the same area of consciousness as James, Stevens pursues the elusive visionary center from the beginning to the end of his career.

For James and Stevens, invoking as final the fleeting moments of perception contradicts the nature of a world in process. Stevens establishes that just as the position of the center implies perceptions from points along the edge, so too the poem of the whole must be defined by the composite of its parts:

> The central poem is the poem of the whole,
> The poem of the composition of the whole,
> The composition of blue sea and of green,
> Of blue light and of green, as lesser poems,
> And the miraculous multiplex of lesser poems,
> Not merely into a whole, but a poem of
> The whole, the essential compact of the parts,
> The roundness that pulls tight the final ring.
>
> (CP 442)

In order to achieve an "essential compact of the parts," the imagination must pursue reality relentlessly, creating through language abstractions of what it sees. It must yield not to the supremacy of the abstractions it creates, but to a constant pressure to decreate and start the process over. Only in this fashion can the poet guarantee himself a claim on the center, for then only does he become not a previous, but a "latest" free man, apt creator-substitute for the defunct gods:

> It was how he was free. It was how his freedom came.
> It was being without description, being an ox.
> It was the importance of the trees outdoors,
> The freshness of the oak-leaves, not so much
> That they were oak-leaves, as the way they looked.
> It was everything being more real, himself
> At the centre of reality, seeing it.
> It was everything bulging and blazing and big in itself.
>
> (CP 205)

The gradual spiritual deflation extending from Emerson's day to the present provides opportunities not for despair but for freedom and hope. Robbed of two "fond old enormities," as E. A. Robinson refers to heaven and hell, and abandoned to a cosmos comprising a "jovial hullabaloo" of "supreme fictions" and engendered truths, James and Stevens project a positive philosophy by which they can balance the burden of nonteleological existence. To Robinson's rhetorical challenge in "The Man Against the Sky," "If there be nothing after Now, And we be nothing anyhow, / And we know that,—why live?"[15] Stevens counsels that with a "mind of winter," man beholds the void with the knowledge that death ends all, but instead of disparaging his plight, he distinguishes between the "Nothing that is not there and the nothing that is" (CP 10), deriving satisfaction from imaginative acts, which, by locating delineations in the subtleties of "nothing," make life worthwhile.

A final consideration in illustrating common theses in the writings of Emerson, James, and Stevens concerns the subject-object—or, as James preferred to call it—the concept-percept relationship. Emerson early recognized that the classic concept of a dualism existing between subject and object, the one totally and ever separate from the other, was not acceptable. He postulated instead an irresolvable tension between them. The subject does not simply perceive the world of object, but by perceiving it, helps to create it. He relinquishes the traditional subject-object split and replaces it with the idea of perpetual interrelation of the one with the other—stimulus affecting response, response shaping stimulus. "Thus inevitably does the universe wear our color, and every object fall successively into the subject itself" (CWE III 79). He explains in "The Poet" that the role of thought is to make things "fit for use," converting the base and the obscene to the illustrious. Because "every hour and change corresponds to and authorizes a different state of the mind" (CWE I 9), nature as object becomes "a vast trope" and the impressions it makes on the imagination "make the great days of life" (CWE VIII 15). The constant interaction of phenomenal reality with imagination and imagination with that reality, Emerson describes dramatically in terms of nature and thought:

History is the action and reaction of these two,—Nature and Thought; two boys pushing each other on the curbstone of the pavement. Everything is pusher or pushed; and matter and mind are in perpetual tilt and balance, so. Whilst the man is weak, the earth takes up him. He plants his brain and affections. By and by he will take up the earth, and have his gardens and vineyards in the beautiful order and productiveness of his thought. Every solid in the universe is ready to become fluid on the approach of the mind, and the power to flux it is the measure of the mind. If the wall remain adamant, it accuses the want of thought. (CWE VI 43)

Emerson here attests not only to the intricate interdependence of mind and reality but to the mind's decreative powers as well. By assuring the fluidity of the universe, the mind avoids the inertia of commitment to rigid systems.

Subject and object in the image of two boys pushing each other on the sidewalk become, for Stevens, the chase of bucks and a firecat. In "Earthy Anecdote," the first poem of The Collected Poems, Stevens, like Emerson, establishes the endless action and reaction of imagination and reality:

> Every time the bucks went clattering
> Over Oklahoma
> A firecat bristled in the way.

(CP 3)

The vaunting clatter of reality in the image of Oklahoma's spirited bucks swerved in "a swift, circular line" to the right and left wherever they went, but could not escape the bristling firecat of imagination. The emphasis is on "Every time." Stevens establishes the true pitch of the relationship since neither force actively pursues the other, yet the parallel arcs of their movement make confrontation inevitable. Wherever the bucks clattered, "The firecat went leaping." Stevens allows that imagination might sleep to reality ("Later, the firecat closed his bright eyes / And slept"), but sleep is an interim; upon awakening, the bucks will make the cat leap again. The boundaries of the chase are endless.

William James discards the subject-object split as categorically as Emerson and Stevens. He asserts that conception is not the higher way to truth over perception, that if conception is not rooted in perception, it is nothing but empty abstraction and fixity. Pragmatism tests the truth and importance of conceptions by relating them back to the perceived reality from which they came. In the *Adagia*, Stevens expresses the same tenet: "Poetry has to be something more than a conception of the mind. It has to be a revelation of nature. Conceptions are artificial. Perceptions are essential" (OP 164).

James recognizes that on a practical level common sense will always contrast "thoughts" and "things," but that philosophically they represent arbitrary classifications, not "what an experience is aboriginally made of" (ERE 272). Man cannot know if the world exists by itself because "for us it is exclusively an object of experience." Therefore, he concludes that "our sensations are not small inner duplicates of things, they are the things themselves in so far as the things are presented to us" (ERE 186). James acknowledges that concepts, however abstract, are as real as percepts for we can never for a moment deny them, but his vital conclusion on the matter relates him specifically to Stevens when he states that "the 'eternal' kind of being [concepts] enjoy is inferior to the temporal kind, because it is so static and schematic and lacks so many characters which temporal reality possesses" (SPP 254). Precisely for this reason Stevens insists that the poet absolve himself from the old fictions, the "eternal concepts," and recreate the world through the vitality of the as-yet-to-be-abstracted percepts in the flux of reality. Realizing the inevitability of creating a schema of concepts, he desires nevertheless, to write a poetry of percepts by which he can escape the tendency to solidify his temporal reality. Stevens illustrates the ramifications of this dilemma in his essay "Honors and Acts." Caught between percept and concept, the poet must realize, Stevens writes, that "the imagination is false, whatever else may be said of it, and reality is true" (OP 241). He means that the imagination's versions do not duplicate reality but create fictions that merely approximate it and, in the nature of abstractions, falsify it. Conceptions falsify the perceptions from which they issue. Nevertheless, Stevens affirms that the poet gains in the process since the activities of imagination immerse him in the particulars of his world:

being concerned that poetry should be a thing of vital and virile importance, [the poet] commits himself to reality, which then becomes his
inescapable and ever-present difficulty and inamorata. In any event, he
has lost nothing; for the imagination, while it might have led him to
purities beyond definition, never yet progressed except by particulars.
Having gained the world, the imaginative remains available to him in
respect to all the particulars of the world. Instead of having lost anything, he has gained a sense of direction and a certainty of understanding. (OP 241)

James realizes the extent to which language becomes intricately
involved in the subject-object issue. When man pays attention to
the particulars within the flux of matter, he uses language to
name and identify them, thus creating "concepts" of them: "Out
of time we cut 'days' and 'nights,' 'summers' and 'winters.' We
say *what* each part of the sensible continuum is, and all these ab-
stracted *whats* are concepts" (SPP 234). The intellectual life of
man, then, consists in substituting concepts for the percepts of
which his experience originates. Like bucks and firecat, they are
inseparable: "percepts and concepts interpenetrate and melt together, impregnate and fertilize each other. Neither, taken alone,
knows reality in its completeness. We need them both, as we
need both our legs to walk with" (SPP 235). As the medium of
communication, language arbitrates the subject-object dynamism.

For Emerson, since "words are signs of natural facts" (CWE I
25), language embodies in words the mind's perception of reality: "The world being thus put under the mind for verb and noun,
the poet is he who can articulate it" (CWE III 20). Poets, he
continues, made all the words and "each word was at first a stroke
of genius" because to the first speaker and hearer it "symbolized
the world." The poet earns the right to name things because he
comes nearer to the world than others. Emerson posits what he
calls a "radical correspondence between visible things and human
thoughts" (CWE I 29). Man uses language to convert external
phenomena—or visible things—into verbal figures. Emerson associates language with man's need to utter truth: "A man's power to
connect his thought with its proper symbol, and so to utter it, de-

pends on the simplicity of his character, that is, upon his love of truth and his desire to communicate it without loss" (CWE I 29). He warns, however, that language easily follows upon the corruption of men who use it for duplicity and falsehood and cease to create new imagery. "In due time," he asserts, ". . . words lose all power to stimulate the understanding of the affections" and writers, proclaiming to utter truth, do nothing but "feed unconsciously on the language created by the primary writers of the country" (CWE I 30). Emerson also realizes that the paradox of language is that it deadens the very reality to which it originally gave life: "every sentence . . . hath some falsehood of exaggeration in it. For the infinite diffuseness refuses to be epigrammatized, the world to be shut in a word. The thought being spoken in a sentence becomes by mere detachment falsely emphatic" (EJ VIII 87).

Although Stevens, like Emerson, recognized that "The words of things entangle and confuse" (CP 41) and that the world will long survive the poems written about it, he knew that "words . . . are life's voluble utterance" (CP 188), and that "there is no life except in the word of it" (CP 287). Words are the modern poet's means of mediating between himself and insignificance. Stevens' interest rests as much with the music of words as with their meaning. "Words," he says, "are the only melodeon" (OP 171). By blending meaning and sound in infinite variety, language continually undergoes and expresses change; it partakes, therefore, of the very process that it describes. Since the mind also operates within its own flux, words become the appropriate means for the poet to express thoughts and feelings. So long as the poet uses words as a means of articulating flux, he will not submit to the tendency of words to tyrannize reality by fixing it. Stevens emphasizes that language is "the material of poetry not its mere medium or instrument" (OP 171). Also, he remarks that "in the world of words, the imagination is one of the forces of nature" (OP 170). Through words, the imagination creates fictions sufficient to sustain man at the creative center of his universe. "On a few words of what is real in the world / I nourish myself," Stevens writes, and in "The Noble Rider and Sound of Words," he explains the sense in which words nourish:

The deepening need for words to express our thoughts and feelings which, we are sure, are all the truth that we shall ever experience, having no illusions, makes us listen to words when we hear them, loving them and feeling them, makes us search the sound of them, for a finality, a perfection, an unalterable vibration, which it is only within the power of the acutest poet to give them. . . . Poetry is a revelation in words by means of words." (NA 32–33)

Words replace God and immortality as man's sole hope for locating finality and perfection. Joseph Riddel rightly notices that for Stevens words not only "give shape to the clutter of things," but, more importantly, they "establish the discreet primacy of mind over things."[16]

The philosophy of William James stipulates the function of language in a pragmatic world and clarifies Stevens' concept of words. When Stevens asserts that "Words add to the senses" (CP 234) and when he answers the question "What is it that my feeling seeks?" with "It wants words" (CP 207), he returns to James's contention that each letter of the alphabet and every part of speech attaches itself to feelings: "There is not a conjunction or a preposition, and hardly an adverbial phrase, syntactic form, or inflection of voice, in human speech, that does not express some shading or other of relation which we at some moment actually feel to exist between the larger objects of our thought" (PP 38). Since words are the aspects of our experience that are "revivable as actual sensations more easily than any other items" (PP 54), then each word uttered provokes a *feeling* of the sensible continuity of life that it strives to portray. James concludes, therefore, that "we ought to say a feeling of *and*, a feeling of *if*, a feeling of *but*, and a feeling of *by*, quite as readily as we say a feling of *blue* or a feeling of *cold*" (PP 38). Just as no single aspect of the flux touches the mind of man outside of those aspects that precede and follow it, so also, no single word in a sentence touches consciousness as simply a noise. The process of language then must be aligned to the process of the world. We feel the meaning of a word as it passes, James says, and "in our feeling of each word there chimes an echo or foretaste of every other. The consciousness of the 'Idea' and that of the words are thus consubstantial" (PP 67).

The feelings of words uniting with the feelings of objects create a situation of intense perceptive dynamism. In poems early and late, Stevens writes as one keenly aware of the intricate union of the processes of the world on the one hand and the processes of language on the other. By expressing new feelings with new words and new syntactic structures, Stevens becomes, like the lady by the sea in Key West, "the single artificer" of the world in which he walks. He absorbs the motion of the world into himself and, out of the interaction of object with subject in continuing process, creates the vital forms that carry him forward to fresh perception. Since "The imperfect is our paradise" in a pluralistic universe, then delight lies "in flawed words and stubborn sounds" (CP 194). The poems of Wallace Stevens manifest in dramatic ways what happens when the consciousness of man conjures sufficient bravado to say "I am" to the void, then takes upon itself the challenge of decorating the emptiness in the streamers of his own imaginative brilliance. To such a one, the "theory of description matters most" because it is the "theory of the word for those / For whom the word is the making of the world" (CP 345). This, for Stevens, is the basis of fictive language.

Through words as expressions of the mind's acts, Stevens makes a place for his imagination most fully to be. He creates not out of desperation or depression, but out of affirmation. He realizes that "When the phantoms are gone and the shaken realist / First sees reality," the act of perception is itself enough to sustain all affirmations since it sustains the "passion for yes that had never been broken" (CP 320). The words of philosophers and poets, says James, "give you somewhere to go from . . . a direction and a place to reach" (CER 347). For the philosopher-poet Stevens, a fictitious existence on an exquite plane comprises both the direction and the place to reach of poetry; and the imagination is the only "somewhere" from which anyone can proceed.

Toward Decreation
and the Supreme Fiction

n "The Sentiment of Rationality," William James argues that a man's philosophic attitude is determined
by how he balances two antithetical cravings—the
"passion for simplification," whereby man resolves
the diversity of the world into harmony and simplicity, and the opposing "passion for distinguishing," which cares little for the harmony of the whole, preferring instead familiarity with the parts.
The "passion for simplification" is characterized by the need
to know things by their causes and to reduce the world's complexity to fundamental laws and relationships. The "passion for
distinguishing" is characterized by loyalty to integrity of perception and dislike of vague identifications. "It loves to recognize
particulars in their full completeness," James elaborates, "and the
more of these it can carry the happier it is. It prefers any amount
of incoherence, abruptness, and fragmentariness (so long as the
literal details of the separate facts are saved)" (WB 319). Because no system of philosophy that violates either need can ever
be universally acceptable, James concludes that the only possible
philosophy must be a compromise—"between an abstract monot-
ony and a concrete heterogeneity" (WB 319).

In Stevens the "passion for distinguishing" surges unchecked,
while many would argue that a balancing "passion for simplification" does not exist in him. Subscribing to the notion of a fluid
world, he prefers the fragmentary to the harmonious, the discursive to the precise, and he composes often impenetrable, seem-
ingly incoherent poems. His interest centers on the variations and

nuances of the world in its manifold parts and on the clarity by which he perceives those parts. "Accuracy of observation is the equivalent of accuracy of thinking," he writes in the *Adagia* (OP 158). And again, "the notion of absolutes is relative" (OP 158). Clearly, his poetry veers away from tendencies to generalize, resolve, or simplify. While he confesses that "the individual partakes of the whole," he denies—"except in extraordinary cases"— that the individual can add to the whole (OP 161).

Then how does the prerequisite "passion for simplification" express itself in Stevens? James stipulates that "the only way to mediate between diversity and unity is to class the diverse items as cases of a common essence which you discover in them" (WB 319–20). Emerson makes a similar point when he avers that as the mind submits to its unifying instinct "classification begins" (CWE I 85). For one who subscribes to a chaotic universe, the craving for harmony must be satisfied by the processes through which the chaos is distilled. In Stevens' case, these processes are poems, melodic interludes of order in the chaotic flux. He classifies the diverse items of his world in the "common essence" of the poetic act. Writing poetry satisfies the "blessed rage for order" (CP 130) or the "passion for simplification." Poetry then becomes a means by which he incorporates the diversity of the pluralistic world into an harmonious medium.

But the achievement of harmony is as fleeting as the acts of the mind from which the harmonizing poems emanate. No sooner has the rage for order yielded the classifying medium—the poem— than the opposing rage for chaos, the "passion for distinguishing," reasserts itself. A new and different world flows by and the poet's mind flows after it. "It is not every day that the world arranges itself in a poem" (OP 165), Stevens assures. Anticipating a principal theme in "Notes Toward a Supreme Fiction," James reminds that a system of classification "must always be abstract, since the basis of every classification is the abstract essence embedded in the living fact,—the rest of the living fact being for the time ignored by the classifier" (WB 320). In Stevens' case, to ignore the living fact is to frustrate the "passion for distinguishing," the craving that compels him to attune his imagination to the parts of the processive world currently before him, not to the parts classified already either in his own poems or in someone else's. Stevens subscribes fully to James's conclusion that although the classification of things is, on the one hand, "the best possible theoretic philosophy," ·on the other, it is "a most miserable and inadequate substitute for the fullness of the truth. It is a monstrous abridgment of life, which, like all abridgments is got by the absolute loss and casting out of real matter" (WB 321).

The implications of this discussion are important because they establish a base for understanding Stevens' concepts of process and decreation, and for the gradual development of his "ephebe," or young poet—a manifestation of Emerson's "scholar"—who appears repeatedly in Stevens' first three books. Realizing with James and Emerson that conceptions are teleological instruments, Stevens fashions a theory of poetry through which the imagination first releases reality from old conceptions—the old teleological instruments—before it gratifies its need to simplify reality by conceptualizing it within fresh imaginative acts. As a scholar of his universe he perceives reality directly instead of parroting other men's perceptions of it and so avoids the degenerate state of society that Emerson deplores in "The American Scholar" in which "the members have suffered amputation from the trunk, and strut about so many walking monsters" (CWE I 83). In his essay "The Relations between Poetry and Painting," Stevens clarifies the point: "modern reality is a reality of decreation, in which our revelations are not the revelations of belief, but the precious portents of our own powers" (NA 175). The modern poet invokes the power of his mind to disengage himself from sterile belief and to rely on immediate insight.

Stevens' first three books chart a gradual movement toward self-discovery and self-reliance achieved by decreating the world of fixity to discover its vibrant core. Manifestations of Emerson's American scholar permeate these early poems. Reformulating Emerson's notion of the poetic office to ply "the slow, unhonored, and unpaid task of observation" (CWE I 100), Stevens' scholar-as-poet becomes an "introspective voyager" (CP 29) en route to the center of his cosmos.

Unmistakably, Stevens aligns himself to the same world of multiplicity, disorder, and change to which both Emerson and James subscribe. The poems of *Harmonium*, Stevens' first collection, are those of a younger man whose developing philosophy brings him gradually to the conclusion that his imagination is the single fulcrum in the chaos of reality, his poems the sole arbiters of how the world exists in the moment-to-moment of perception. They reflect a narrator testing new belief, adjusting himself to the fearsome independence of his new reality and to the awesome role of his craft. At this early stage, however, Stevens reveals considerable hesitation at having to assume a role as artificer of a fluxional world. While several poems evoke a confident and composed narrator delighting in the flowing particulars of his world, others reveal just the opposite. The ephebe who emerges in gradual stages through three later poems—"The Comedian as the Letter C," "The Man with the Blue Guitar," and "Notes Toward a Supreme Fiction"—is barely discernible in many of the *Harmonium* poems.

In "Dominations of Black," the processive world becomes too much for the speaker comfortably to bear. The poem begins with a deceptively peaceful image. A speaker sits tranquilly by the fireside in a comfortable microcosm:

> At night, by the fire,
> The colors of the bushes
> And of the fallen leaves,
> Repeating themselves,
> Turned in the room,
> Like the leaves themselves
> Turning in the wind.

>   (CP 8)

The speaker discerns shapes in the leap of flames, but his mind-game suddenly gets out of hand and he becomes trapped in an imaginative room of his own structuring. In the reds and oranges of the fire, the narrator recalls the colored leaves flying in the autumn wind. Then the imagination assumes its own fluxional mode and becomes a darting eye focusing upon the specters in nature's train:

> I heard them cry—the peacocks.
> Was it a cry against the twilight
> Or against the leaves themselves
> Turning in the wind,
> Turning as the flames
> Turned in the fire,
> Turning as the tails of the peacocks
> Turned in the loud fire.
>
> (CP 9)

Caught in the imprecision of shifting imaginings, the whirling of reality's wheel overcomes the diminutive perceiver. His comforting microcosm by the fireside succumbs to the awesome macrocosm—in this case, as much the evocation of a mind-in-process as an objective rendering of the world-in-process:

> Out of the window,
> I saw how the planets gathered
> Like the leaves themselves
> Turning in the wind.
> I saw how the night came,
> Came striding like the color of the heavy hemlocks
> I felt afraid.
> And I remembered the cry of the peacocks.
>
> (CP 9)

In a stream of association, the perceiver dresses reality in his own private nightmare: he is afraid to die. He shifts the need to scream out against the narrowing vortex of change, darkness, and death to the peacocks whose remembered cry temporarily subdues him. He sits in the guise of a pure imagination submissive to wherever reality wishes to take it. His commitment to reality's "gorgeous wheel" (CP 121) permits the exquisite grace in the movement of the lines and imagery yet does little to avert the pain of realizing his insignificance in the orderless flux.

Stevens' depression never becomes a pervasive tone. Playful

poems quickly offset those of darker moods. The poet of *Harmonium* contemplates a world-in-process and the range of moods in his poems expresses the happy-sad extremes of such a world. In 1922, he lamented to Harriet Monroe that "gathering together the things for my book has been so depressing"; and he suggested that all his early works "seem like horrid cocoons from which later abortive insects have sprung. The book will amount to nothing, except that it may teach me something" (LWS 231). The later poems testify that his first book taught Stevens much; the early cocoons did not bear abortive fruit. However, the compendium of moods and flourishes in *Harmonium* indicates that he was wrestling with the implications of embracing a philosophy of restlessness and flux, that he had discovered with James that "the pluralism and the restlessness are repugnant and irrational in a certain way"; yet, also with James, he knew that every alternative to them was "irrational in a deeper way" (WB 606).

Poem after poem in *Harmonium* bears witness to the positive side of commitment to a fluid world. In "Life Is Motion," a poem of process in its purist and simplest state, Stevens celebrates a couple dancing in a manner reminiscent of William Carlos Williams opening a refrigerator door and enjoying the simple, unrestrictive pleasure of tasting cold plums. The poem describes in nine short lines an Oklahoma couple, Bonnie and Josie, dressed in calico, dancing around a stump:

> They cried,
> "Ohoyaho,
> Ohoo" . . .
> Celebrating the marriage
> Of flesh and air.

$$(CP\ 83)$$

In its primitive simplicity, "Life Is Motion" anticipates what later becomes a more complex form of decreation. Like Williams, Stevens stresses that one must regain the ability to appreciate so basic a spectacle as simple beings dancing.

Stevens' more difficult poems depicting process illustrate that the fluxional nature of the external world contributes to the mind's activity; external process vitalizes internal process resulting in poems as restless as the flux itself. In "The Wind Shifts," Stevens uses a series of similes to illustrate how vibrations in the world relate to vibrations of the mind. The wind shifts "Like the thoughts of an old human," "Like a human without illusions," "Like humans approaching proudly," "Like humans approaching angrily," "Like a human, heavy and heavy" (CP 83–84). Metaphor for the spinning world, the wind shifts directions as arbitrarily as the mind and moods of man. By extension, Stevens implies that when the world shifts, the mind shifts with it endlessly, recalling the perpetual chase of bucks and firecat (reality and imagination) in "Earthy Anecdote."

Probably the most important of the poems depicting process in *Harmonium* is "Sea Surface Full of Clouds." Like "Thirteen Ways of Looking at a Blackbird" and "Six Significant Landscapes," "Sea Surface" exemplifies what James calls the "additive constitution" of the world. Each of the three poems divides into several cantos—the number could be infinite—each division relating to one another because of the ordering prevalency of the imagination. "It *may* be," says James, "that some parts of the world are connected so loosely with some other parts as to be strung along by nothing but the copula *and*. They might even come and go without those other parts suffering any internal change" (PR 418).

In "Sea Surface," the narrator recalls impressions garnered on the deck of a ship "In that November off Tehuantepec" (CP 98). Stevens strings together five renditions of the remembered experience—each canto incrementally adjusting details of the previous, adding nuances that could be added endlessly according to the imagination's vigor. Stevens deftly manipulates what for him is a rigid pattern (six tercets per canto, each opening with approximately the same two lines) without destroying the impression of an imagination in the act of ordering a free-flowing experience:

> In that November off Tehuantepec,
> The slopping of the sea grew still one night
> And in the morning summer hued the deck

> And made one think of rosy chocolate
> And gilt umbrellas. Paradisal green
> Gave suavity to the perplexed machine
>
> Of ocean, which like limpid water lay.
>
> (CP 98–99)

The developing sequences illustrate the Emersonian-Jamesian theory that reality changes as the mind perceiving it changes. The "paradisal green" of the first canto transposes in the next six cantos into "sham-like green," "uncertain green," "too-fluent green," and so on. Recalling an additive experience, the imagination connects the disparate parts—inserts "the copula *and*"—and processes the vibrancies of the event for the perceiver. In the final canto, the imaginative ordering of a remembered experience abruptly ends at a point where it could as easily have continued:

> Then the sea
> And heaven rolled as one and from the two
> Came fresh transfigurings of freshest blue.
>
> (CP 102)

If the imagination chose to pursue the "fresh transfigurings," the poem would move through further adumbrations of green and chocolate.

Ronald Sukenick notices that "Sea Surface Full of Clouds" presents five ways of looking at a seascape; it differs from "Thirteen Ways of Looking at a Blackbird" only in the sense that, while the sea is a constant in the former poem, the blackbird's implication changes within each of the thirteen contexts in which it appears.[1] Both poems, however, illustrate the processive activity of what Sukenick aptly calls the "proliferating imagination." William James discusses this complex interrelationship of mind and object acting in process in his essays "The Stream of Thought" and "On the Notion of Reality as Changing," and he provides a graphic illustration of what happens in Stevens' poems depicting process. "In every series of real terms," he writes, "not only do the terms themselves and their associates and environments change, but we change, and their *meaning* for us changes, so that new kinds of sameness and types of causation continually come into view and appeal to our interest" (PU 301). Clearly, the meaning of the blackbird changes within each context in which Stevens places it, just as the vocabulary and even the syntax by means of which he describes "that November off Tehuantepec" become crucial aspects of the evolving remembrance of clouds reflecting in the sea's surface. The drift of the mind over objects stimulates verbal description, which, in turn, alters the direction of the drifting mind. James argues that "the transition between the thought of one object and the thought of another is no more a break in the *thought* than a joint in a bamboo is a break in the wood" (PP 34). In precise, technical description, James focuses Stevens' procedure in poems like "Sea Surface Full of Clouds" and "Thirteen Ways of Looking at a Blackbird":

If recently the brain-tract a was vividly excited, and then b, and now vividly c, the total present consciousness is not produced simply by c's excitement, but also by the dying vibrations of a and b as well . . . three different processes coexisting, and correlated with them a thought which is no one of the three thoughts which they would have produced had each of them occurred alone. But whatever this fourth thought may exactly be, it seems impossible that it should not be something *like* each of the three other thoughts whose tracts are concerned in its production, though in a fast-waning phase. (PP 35–36)

In James's terms, retracing the experience at Tehuantepec excites brain tracts a through e while imaginative concentration on the figure of a blackbird stimulates consecutive brain tracts a through m. Each subsequent imaginative utterance correlates to what precedes it; as the mind operates within the flux of its own procedure, it responds to the "dying vibrations" of its own series of consecutive acts. Sukenick rightly observes that the figure of the blackbird "does not have a constant signification but it has a constant function: to act as a focus that brings out qualities in what is put in relation with it."[2] As the imagination focuses reality's flux, the blackbird focuses the process of the imagination's activity.

Stevens' experiments in the lineaments of process gradually bring him to a theory of a central self whose perceptions could

supplant all other concepts of the world. He becomes more convinced of the imagination's power, recognizing, as he wrote in
"Imagination as Value," that "it enables us to live our own lives.
We have it because we do not have enough without it" (NA
150). He advances Emerson's theme in "The American Scholar,"
that "in going down into the secrets of his own mind [the scholar]
has descended into the secrets of all minds" (CWE I 103).
Occasionally, the emergence of the central perceiving narrator is
accompanied by playful self-ridicule, as if Stevens feels the need
to poke fun at the bravado of his own overly confident narrator.
"Ploughing on Sunday" depicts a speaker brazenly asserting the
rights of his imagination not only to be in reality, but to shout
about it:

> Remus, blow your horn!
> I'm ploughing on Sunday,
> Ploughing North America.
> Blow your horn!

(CP 20)

Since the poet sings and ploughs on Sunday, the day for rest and
worship in the Christian myth, Daniel Fuchs conceives this poem
as an "exuberantly jocular . . . assault on tradition," in which a
blaspheming narrator flaunts a new role for the perceiving imagination in witness to a spiritually unsponsored reality.[3] A narrator
of similar exuberance in "Bantams in Pine-Woods" again mocks
tradition, this time in the form of the stilted, conservative type of
savior-poet—the "ten-foot poet among inchlings"—who presumes
reality to be the servant of his own creativity and projects himself
as the voice of the multitude:

> Damned universal cock, as if the sun
> Was blackamoor to bear your blazing tail.
>
> Fat! Fat! Fat! Fat! I am the personal.
> Your world is you. I am my world.

(CP 75)

The subdued narrator of "Sunday Morning" manifests one so
convinced of his commitment to a pluralistic world that he can

depend upon an argument proceeding from the parts themselves
to make his point. The Christian woman in the poem suggests a
feminine version of Stevens' ephebe-scholar, who must learn a
fundamental lesson before she can appreciate fully the lusciousness
of her world. Edward Kessler notices the bisexuality of
Stevens' imagination and considers the recurrence of the female
figure as manifesting one side of man's essential duality between
reason (male) and passion (female).[4] The male narrator in "Sunday
Morning" represents a maturer version of the teacher-at-the-
center whose perceptions of reality are not modified by any of the
woman's traditional categories. "Sunday Morning" restates Emerson's
contention that the man of the world "is a realist, and converses
with things" (CWE I 157). More significantly, it elaborates,
in miniature, James's philosophy of pragmatism.

The lesson the narrator offers the woman reiterates the pragmatic
message that she must avoid abstraction, insufficiency, fixed
principles, and closed systems, and turn toward concreteness and
fact:

> Why should she give her bounty to the dead?
> What is divinity if it can come
> Only in silent shadows and in dreams?
> Shall she not find in comforts of the sun,
> In pungent fruit and bright, green wings, or else
> In any balm or beauty of the earth,
> Things to be cherished like the thought of heaven?
>
> (CP 67)

In a living and splendid present, why should anyone remove himself
from the richness of luxury within nature's flux and commit
himself instead to the mythy shadows of a transempirical heaven?
James stipulates: "only in so far as they lead us, successfully or
unsuccessfully, back into sensible experience again, are our abstracts
and universals true or false at all" (ERE 218). Stevens'
narrator challenges the legitimacy of the woman's universals, repeatedly
offsetting images of hollow spiritual categories with lush
imagery of a vibrant physical world. The woman's reveries of the
"holy hush" of the crucifixion diffuse into the concrete realities of

a plush nightgown, pungent oranges, coffee, the bright wings of a bird in a pattern in a rug. Joseph Riddel labels the narrator's assertion—"Divinity must live within herself" (CP 67)—as a "latter-day Emersonianism without its transcendental rationale."[5] Indeed, the statement exhorts self-reliance; the rationale of the entire poem, if not transcendental, is certainly pragmatic. The "comforts of the sun" the narrator proposes as replacements for commitment to Christianity's "silent shadows" encompass what James calls "the open air and possibilities of nature," (PR 379) which include the negative as well as the positive fruits of living in a fluid world. Stevens highlights both extremes of the divinity the woman will find by living in herself:

> Passions of rain, or moods in falling snow;
> Grievings in loneliness, or unsubdued
> Elations when the forest blooms; gusty
> Emotions on wet roads on autumn nights;
> All pleasures and all pains, remembering
> The bough of summer and the winter branch.
> These are the measures destined for her soul.
>
> (CP 67)

The lesson for the woman requires that if she is to achieve the full freedom of living in an empirical world that is both sacred and holy, she must attend to the moments of the mind's perception of her luscious surroundings. Happiness issues from the impermanence of seasonal flow, not from a fixed paradise beyond the imagination's reach. Within cyclical time, the woman enjoys and suffers much as the bough of summer becomes the winter branch and the certainty of these cycles provide her the only paradise she needs. By examining the cycles of nature, she learns the cycles of self and realizes that the various myths of afterlife are completely alien to the life of a dynamic self in the natural world. The narrator indicates that man's need for "some imperishable bliss" (CP 68) emanates from an improper understanding of the cyclical thrust of the world as well as of the mind. Since death makes life and beauty happen, man's quest for eternal life represents an utter contradiction. In a world of flux, death becomes not a passage to a fixed heaven where fruit never falls and boughs "hang always heavy" in a perfect sky, but a facet of the procedure of existence and the natural culmination of life's process. Realizing death, man embraces life more fully.

Having learned her lesson, the woman lays aside her Christianity in perceiving that Jesus was not *the Christ* but simply a great man living like herself within the pluralism of natural existence. Taking death away from man, the Christ took life too by substituting "silent shadows" and "dreams" for the vivid particulars of empirical living. When the woman sees the tomb in Palestine as merely "the grave of Jesus, where he lay" (CP 70), she recommits herself to earthly reality. The transformation of the Christ-God to Jesus-man conforms to James's notion that radical empiricism, by discarding the concepts of an absolute "all-form" and embracing instead the "each-forms" makes of God "only one of the eaches" (PU 497).

In "Sunday Morning" Stevens offers nonteleological revelation as a substitute for other inventions of eternity. The narrator's advice to the Christian lady reconstitutes Emerson's advice to the divinity school students: "let the breath of new life be breathed by you through the forms already existing. For if once you are alive, you shall find they shall become plastic and new" (CWE I 150). The woman must embrace the forms of her world as they emanate from her own perception. In so doing, she will replace the desolate Christian mythology with a fiction of her own more sacred than what she lost. Stevens relinquishes the blasphemous narrator's chant he had used in "Ploughing on Sunday" and replaces it with the deliberate statements of a narrator committed to a world holier than the one proposed in the Christian myth. The ring of men chanting in orgy to the sun as a naked source inverts the procedure of Christianity, in which man reaches toward paradise in humble supplication. In Stevens' version, man chants not to but from paradise, not in supplication but in triumph, projecting himself from the center of his universe outward toward the void: "Their chant shall be a chant of paradise, / Out of their blood, returning to the sky" (CP 70). This reverses the

New Testament pattern of Christ returning to earth as "the word made flesh." The paradise gained includes in its multiplicity the essential counterparts of the paradise lost—lord, angels, choir, and heavenly fellowship:

> And in their chant shall enter, voice by voice,
> The windy lake wherein their lord delights,
> The trees, like serafin, and echoing hills,
> That choir among themselves long afterward.
> They shall know well the heavenly fellowship
> Of men that perish and of summer morn.
>
> (CP 70)

Life in the new paradise, however "unsponsored" and "inescapable" it may be, increases for man the possibilities of freedom and hope because it redeems reality by exorcising the absolute. The poem proposes James's "mosaic philosophy" or philosophy of "plural facts" as replacement for a philosophy of wholeness and universals. It requires of man, as Emerson had insisted, that he become central, not extraneous, and that he submit himself to the spontaneous delight of a processive reality. Essentially, the theology Stevens advances in "Sunday Morning" stresses the fundamental pragmatic principle that if an abstract truth does not express itself as a difference in concrete fact, it collapses to insignificance. The woman of the poem must submit her doctrine to the test of concrete reality before continuing a life of dogmatic posturing. In other words, she must avoid the blindness Stevens attributes to the creator in "Negation":

> Hi! The creator too is blind,
> Struggling toward his harmonious whole,
> Rejecting intermediate parts.
>
> (CP 97)

James exclaims in *Pragmatism* that "the earth of things, long thrown into shadow by the glories of the upper ether, must resume its rights" (PR 404). In this philosophical tradition Stevens composed "Sunday Morning" and the entire canon of his poems.

The growth of Stevens' poetic self in *Harmonium* culminates

in "The Comedian as the Letter C," a long poem clearly indicating the extent to which at this early stage of his development
Stevens writes in the bias of Emerson and James. A. Walton Litz
proposes that "The Comedian" "belongs to a familiar literary
genre, the voyage of discovery which becomes an 'introspective'
voyage of self-discovery."[6] Fuchs says the poem is "about the relation of the imaginative man to the natural world."[7] He construes
the fate of Crispin, the poem's richly accoutred persona, as "nothing less than finding a new self, the old self being forgotten
beyond any possibility of recall."[8] In either case, Crispin's journey
constitutes Stevens' comic analysis of a serious subject, namely
how the uprooted self, purged in a post-Darwinian era of the old
romances that once defined its relevance, can rediscover significance and value in aggressive mental acts.

Lamenting that "our age is retrospective" (CWE I 3), Emerson had argued that the thinking man must replace retrospection
with introspection, precisely the predicament Crispin unwittingly
faces as his voyage begins. In a letter to Hi Simons concerning
"The Comedian," Stevens proposes an appropriate mental itiner-
ary for the voyage of a modern self:

I suppose that the way of all mind is from romanticism to realism, to
fatalism and then to indifferentism, unless the cycle re-commences and
the thing goes from indifferentism back to romanticism all over again.
. . . At the moment, the world in general is passing from the fatalism
stage to an indifferent stage: a stage in which the primary sense is a
sense of helplessness. But, as the world is a good deal more vigorous
than most of the individuals in it, what the world looks forward to is a
new romanticism, a new belief. (LWS 350)

Stevens urges then vigorous selves sufficient to discover a vigorous
world. Ultimately, even though "the last distortion of romance /
Forsook the insatiable egotist" (CP 30), Crispin fails this qualification and lets the rich world pass him by. Stevens himself pursues the central journey Crispin abandons.

In an article on "The Comedian" that Stevens greatly admired,
Hi Simons traces the hero's development through seven distinct
stages. From a "juvenile romantic subjectivism" in Bordeaux he

passes through Yucatan to Havana and settles finally in the Carolinas. His subjectivism matures first into "a realism almost without positive content." Then follow stages of "exotic realism,"
"grandiose objectivism," and "disciplined realism." Finally Crispin
marries and begets children and proceeds into the final stage of
"fatalism and skepticism" where Stevens leaves him.[9]

Crispin's excursion traces an allegorical motif that approximates, but does not complete, a circle. Thus, the letter "C"—a
circle "clipped" (CP 46). From a world of fixity in his native
Bordeaux, he voyages to a world of process where he struggles to
strip himself of old mythologies. His challenge requires that he
become an Emersonian scholar in a Jamesian world. A poet in
sentiment, if not in fact, he represents the modern poet who plies
his trade in a world of particulars where social, political, and moral
hierarchies have crumbled. Unable to withstand the disintegration
of his fixed and unreal environment, Crispin creates a new order
to replace the one he lost, then becomes entrapped in it and
never returns to the imagination's life. The procedure by which
he freed himself from fixity itself engenders fixity. Considered as
a whole, "The Comedian" could easily be mistaken for an unre-
stricted attack on American romanticism. Crispin seems a mock-
hero out of the transcendental movement, a reincarnated "transparent eyeball" who, by seeing all, metaphorically goes blind. As
an "inquisitorial botanist" and "Socrates / Of snails" (CP 27–28)
who comes to the Carolinas and builds a cabin better to learn
nature, he parodies Thoreau and the Walden experiment. As a
poet trying unsuccessfully to write songs of self along the open
road of his voyage, he impersonates Whitman and the processive
reality in *Leaves of Grass*. As an introspective sea-adventurer pit-
ting his diminutive identity against leviathan myths like God and
Triton, he faintly echoes Ishmael's voyage of discovery. A document of the self, "The Comedian" is richly suggestive of similar
American literary documents. It reveals Stevens in a tentative
state about the emergence of himself as poet at the center of his
world with the role of founding "a new romanticism" (LWS
350). It will take the imaginative experiments of *Ideas of Order*

to bring him to the point of creating in "The Man with the Blue Guitar" a self who is heroic, central and not to be mocked.

In the first canto of "The Comedian," Crispin's transference from land to sea begins his decreation. A "nincompated peda-gogue" on land, subscribing to the "nota" that "man is the intelli-gence of his soil" (CP 27), Crispin quickly learns he is not the intelligence of the sea. The "C"-"sea" pun yields an important lesson, for Crispin's artificial personality of the land—his prefabri-cated "C"—must discover its authentic source by returning to the essential "sea"—place of the primitive and origin of all life. Safe on land within the fences of his own categories, the pedagogue's narrow eye cannot tabulate the sea's immensity:

> An eye most apt in gelatines and jupes,
> Berries of villages, a barber's eye,
> An eye of land, of simple salad-beds,
> Of honest quilts, the eye of Crispin, hung
> On porpoises, instead of apricots,
> And on silentious porpoises, whose snouts
> Dibbled in waves that were mustachios,
> Inscrutable hair in an inscrutable world.
>
> (CP 27)

This Crispin, who reigned over the petty world on land, now, on the ubiquitous sea, finds himself "washed away by magnitude" (CP 28). The mythology that he had of himself, that he was "principium / And lex" of his cosmos, is by the sea "Blotched out beyond unblotching" (CP 28). Crispin realizes that the self he enveloped within a maze of preconceptions must be set free. The open-formed sea enacts a cleansing ritual:

> The dead brine melted in him like a dew
> Of winter, until nothing of himself
> Remained, except some starker, barer self
> In a starker, barer world. . . .
>
> . . . . .
>   . . . Crispin
> Became an introspective voyager.
>
> (CP 29)

He loses the last distortion of his previous ego-centered self and perceives the primitive wonder of a bare reality he never before saw:

> Here was no help before reality.
> Crispin beheld and Crispin was made new.
> The imagination, here, could not evade,
> In poems of plums, the strict austerity
> Of one vast, subjugating, final tone.

> (CP 30)

Crispin has learned the first lesson of the emancipated self, that to live in a world without imagination is not to live at all. In James's categories, Crispin shifts from rationalist, "meaning your devotee to abstract and eternal principles," to empiricist, "meaning your lover of facts in all their crude variety" (PR 364). He fulfills Emerson's definition of the "true man" who "belongs to no other time or place, but is the centre of things" (CWE II 60). He emerges from a sterile nonreality, a nonpragmatic existence of the kind characterized vividly by James as "some substitute for [reality] which previous human thinking has peptonized and cooked for our consumption. If so vulgar an expression were allowed us, we might say that wherever we find it, it has been already *faked*" (PR 453).

Yet Crispin's is a fledgling self, at best. As "a man made vivid by the sea" (CP 30), he feels replenished by the fresh reality he perceives. In Yucatan the Maya sonneteers ignore the lush particulars of their primitive habitat. Not Crispin. His newest, barest self adheres to particulars. He discovers reality as the imagination's source and vows a new aesthetic and a new poetry. He will confront the primitive world with original eye and will convert the "beautiful barrennesses," the "savagery of palms," into a new paradigm. Yet for all his exuberance, earth's "jostling festival" is more than this fledgling pragmatist can tolerate. "Pluralistic empiricism," James warns, "is a turbid, muddled, gothic sort of an affair, without a sweeping outline" (PU 498). For Crispin, the thunderstorms in Yucatan are gothicism enough. Like the lady in

"Sunday Morning" who in contentment still yearns for the comforts of an old mythology, Crispin, freshly liberated from mythologies, flees to a cathedral in the wake of Yucatan's awesome thunder, blithely ignorant of the irony of his flight:

> Crispin, here, took flight.
> An annotator has his scruples, too.
> He knelt in the cathedral with the rest,
> This connoisseur of elemental fate.

(CP 32)

Up to this point, despite its reductive comical format, Crispin's voyage has been in positive directions. Fundamentally, however, Crispin remains the clown, a passive, almost foolish Sancho Panza, who, instead of charging the windmill, will wait for it to charge him; more appropriately, he will lose his way en route to the conflict and end up exactly where he began—in a closed, suffocating, categorical system. He arrives in Carolina prepared to transform its reality into "The book of moonlight"—poetry's fictions. His new aesthetic, appropriate to Stevens' own, involves "An up and down between two elements, / A fluctuating between sun and moon" (CP 35). Predictably, however, his imagination (moon) runs counter to reality (sun): the Carolina he construed as "polar-purple, chilled / And lank" (CP 34) turns out to be "Irised in dew and early fragrancies" (CP 36), a rancid reality ripe in the life-decay of flux. Crispin remains undaunted. He adjusts himself once more to his recent discovery of process and moves ever inward toward the center of his being:

> He marked the marshy ground around the dock,
> The crawling railroad spur, the rotten fence,
> Curriculum for the marvelous sophomore.
> It purified. It made him see how much
> Of what he saw he never saw at all.
> He gripped more closely the essential prose
> As being, in a world so falsified,
> The one integrity for him.

(CP 36)

His voyage over, Crispin's new self, sea-cleansed, settles again on land. The final three sections of "The Comedian" trace the failure of Crispin's experience. He inverts the "Nota" of his old landlocked philosophy. "Man is the intelligence of his soil," a dogma that subjugated reality to the mind's whim, becomes a premise in which reality forms and controls imagination: "his soil is man's intelligence. / That's better. That's worth crossing seas to find" (CP 36). Having destroyed the last remnant of his old mythology, he plans a colony in which "To make a new intelligence prevail," a place to test the strength of his aesthetic and to contemplate "the reverberations in the words / Of his first central hymns" (CP 37). He has achieved a position at the center, both of himself and of his world. For a brief instant, he is one of those to whom Emerson wrote: "Absolve you to yourself, and you shall have the suffrage of the world" (CWE II 50). In appropriate Emersonian fashion, he projects his own Brook Farm, a commune-colony

> that should extend
> To the dusk of a whistling south below the south,
> A comprehensive island hemisphere.
>
> (CP 38)

At this point, however, the poem's narrator separates himself from Crispin's exploits and sagely rejects Crispin's planned colony as a subconscious effort to recreate the categorical world from which he issued:

> These bland excursions into time to come,
> Related in romance to backward flights,
> However prodigal, however proud,
> Contained in their afflatus the reproach
> That first drove Crispin to his wandering.
>
> (CP 39)

So Crispin casually settles into a comfortable hedonist's life not much different from what he left in Bordeaux. In the tradition of a true hedonist, he acquires things: cabin, "prismy blonde" wife,

and daughters—"four blithe instruments / Of differing struts"
(CP 45). The processive world shrinks to the circumference of his
cabin yard, in which each morning he makes

> a round
> Less prickly and much more condign than that
> He once thought necessary.
>
> (CP 42)

He becomes not radical empiricist in pragmatic world—not one
whose imagination engenders truth upon reality—but brute realist—one for whom "what is is what should be" (CP 41). Imagination routed again, Crispin has learned nothing. He recedes to an
"Effective colonizer sharply stopped / In the door-yard by his
own capacious bloom" (CP 44).

In "The Comedian" Stevens clarifies for himself the direction
he intends his aesthetic theory to take. A surrogate of his creator,
Crispin strips reality of one mythology after the other, striving to
locate Stevens' equivalent of "rock," the savage source of reality's
energy. Yet, while coming as close as he comes, Crispin decides
that reality is enough; it does not require the imagination's ren-
derings. Realizing that "The words of things entangle and confuse" (CP 41), he surrenders writing poetry altogether and re-
pudiates the central power that Emerson and James attribute to
the imagination of man to animate the reality he perceives. Emphatically, Stevens rejects Crispin's option. Steven prefers to continue to create his own world through fictive parables. By creating
in Crispin a somewhat bungling mock-heroic figure of the self,
he achieves the perspective necessary for the continuing evolution
of the confident ephebe that emerges more emphatically in *Ideas
of Order* and especially in "The Man with the Blue Guitar." In
the several years separating *Harmonium* from *Ideas of Order*,
Stevens focuses the disparate roles he had entertained for his
poetic self in his first book and opts for a life of the imagination
dramatically alien to that embraced by Crispin, his autobiographi-
cal counterpart. Riddel offers a pertinent insight here:

Crispin assimilated the various masks of *Harmonium* and neatly trimmed them into a discreet and humble ego. How necessary this pruning of self was to later maturity, subsequent volumes would reveal. But its immediate importance was that it brought the celebrant of the physical world back to that world and freed him from the drift toward solipsism.[10]

Riddel's comment brings this discussion back to Emerson and James. Regardless of the denouement of "The Comedian as the Letter C," and of Crispin specifically, the fact remains that the poem subscribes to a pragmatic vision of the world as well as to the principles for the discovery of the essential self outlined by Emerson in "Self-Reliance" and "The American Scholar." Crispin's clipped redemption occurs at all because he debunks conformity, consistency, and every form of sterility, and tries, to the extent of his powers, to take a central position in the universe and to live in its forms. "The power which resides in [man]," writes Emerson, "is new in nature, and none but he knows what that is which he can do, nor does he know until he has tried" (CWE II 46). Crispin fulfills this maxim. On each part of his voyage, he animates what James calls the "really malleable" world by fictions emanating from his imagination, rendering order to what is otherwise chaotic. Crispin "dwelt in the land" (CP 40). He discovers a pluralistic world, orders it by imaginative acts, and expresses it in language. Yet, after all, neither Emerson nor James nor Stevens himself can abide him. Crispin's cabin, unlike Thoreau's, becomes a prison wherein he extinguishes the imagination's light and loses his hold on a world-in-process.

Itself an aspect of process, Stevens' progression toward the central self is organic and occurs within the logic of his premises. The poems of *Harmonium* indicate that Stevens had some difficulty accepting the inevitable conclusions of these premises. Acknowledging process required destroying fixity, but the removal of fixity's comforting props abandoned the imagination to the single possible position it could occupy in such a world: center. If Crispin sidestepped the challenge, Stevens could not, and its inevitability was disturbing. To achieve a position of relative calm at the center of the chaos, Stevens' ephebe had to come to terms with the stark violence inherent in imaginative acts; he had to learn the extreme to which, through acts of decreation, poetry was a "destructive force" (CP 192). The evidence of the poems suggests that in the intervening years between *Harmonium* and *Ideas of Order*, Stevens learned these lessons.

The manner of Crispin's dissolution signifies Stevens' early consciousness of the violence of decreation. For Crispin to become a "bare self . . . in a barer world," the cosmos of which he was "principium and lex" is drastically dismantled; it implodes within his consciousness. Following this purging of the last distortions of romance, Crispin experiences a "violence . . . for aggrandizement" and searches for a new aesthetic that will be "tough, diverse, untamed" (CP 31). To perceive primitive reality requires imaginative force. But Crispin's aesthetic proves not strong enough to withstand untamed reality. He becomes an accessory, not a center, to nature, the perfect inversion of the condition Emerson proposes for the true scholar. Not until thirteen years after the publication of *Harmonium*, when he published "The Man with the Blue Guitar" and *Ideas of Order*, does Stevens discover what Crispin, as an immature, untempered version of himself, had failed to find—that "tough, untamed, diverse" aesthetic that he embraces as the single opportunity for freedom and optimism in the nonteleological world.

"Farewell to Florida," the initial poem of *Ideas of Order*, reveals the confidence and exuberance of Stevens' new poetic voice:

> Go on, high ship, since now, upon the shore,
> The snake has left its skin upon the floor.
>
> · · · ·
>   . . . The moon
> Is at the mast-head and the past is dead.
> Her mind will never speak to me again.
> I am free.   (CP 117)

Stevens recovers his discarded imagination in the figure of the moon leading the ship away from the past. The voyage motif establishes "Farewell to Florida" as a reenactment, in miniature, of Crispin's trip from Bordeaux—a fitting transition to the new book; only now a maturer mind steers the ship. The imagination of the voyager this time emerges untrammeled by lush reality. Neither comedian nor clown, Stevens' liberated narrator exudes strength and a vigorous commitment to the flux of reality. He departs from the plush South, where Crispin had settled into hedonistic fixity, and proceeds toward a North that is "leafless"— without the dressing of old forms. He prepares to immerse himself into James's turbid pluralism, a processive world in which "a slime of men in crowds / . . . [is] moving as the water moves" (CP 118). Significantly, he welcomes the violence implied in his quest:

> To be free again, to return to the violent mind
> That is their mind, these men, and that will bind
> Me round, carry me, misty deck, carry me
> To the cold, go on, high ship, go on, plunge on.
>
> (CP 118)

Here Stevens indirectly brings forward Emerson's notion of the vitality of impermanence through Walt Whitman. The strong imperatives of "Farewell to Florida" have their source in Whitman's grand tribute to the imagination's life-in-change, "Crossing Brooklyn Ferry":

> Flow on, river! flow on with the flood-tide,
>   and ebb with the ebb-tide!
>
>   . . . .
>
> Come on, ships from the lower bay! pass
>   up or down, white-sail'd schooners,
>   sloops, lighters![11]

Stevens' journey northward parallels the latter half of Crispin's voyage and manifests with particular emphasis his intention to avoid his comedian's degrading denouement.

From this point, the poems enact more serious and distilled demythologizing. "Sad Strains of a Gray Waltz" reiterates total separation from the past. The narrator bluntly admits that "Too many waltzes have ended" (CP 121). The obsolete music of those who "found all form and order in solitude" no longer suffices since "the epic of disbelief / Blares oftener and soon" and "There is order in neither sea nor sun" (CP 121–22). More and more, the multiplicity and chaos console Stevens. In "Autumn Refrain," the speaker realizes that "beneath / The stillness of everything gone . . . / . . . something resides" (CP 160). The sound of the "skrittering residuum" in an utterly decreated world becomes the only fit sound for the imagination to ponder: "And the stillness is in the key, all of it is, / The stillness is all in the key of that desolate sound" (CP 160). Instead of struggling with the crumbling teleologies, Stevens' ephebe bids them good riddance, for he recognizes their paralyzing effect on the imagination's power. "Academic Discourse in Havana" acknowledges that the old "serener" myths involving "nightingales, / Jehovah and the great sea-worm" (CP 142) are no longer able to sustain man; they "Passed like a circus" into oblivion. The contemporary poet—Emerson's "Poet"—must evade such trifles and penetrate beyond them to nature's core:

> As part of nature he [the poet] is part of us.
> His rarities are ours: may they be fit
> And reconcile us to our selves in those
> True reconcilings, dark, pacific words,
> And the adroiter harmonies of their fall.
>
> (CP 144)

As Stevens brings his poetic self closer to the center of the flux, his confident poetic voice resists the temptation to substitute, as Crispin had, new systems of order for those the imagination eliminates by violent decreation. By attuning himself to the elemental "something" that resides after the elimination of fixity, man can satisfy his rage for order by acts of the mind that create not order but "ideas of order"—abstractions of order that issue from the moment-to-moment contact of mind and reality in perpetual correlation. These momentary perceptions are enough to sustain man in the chaos since they provide him with endless opportunities for free action and for renewed intimacy with his changing world.

"The Idea of Order at Key West," considered the "prelude to 'The Man with the Blue Guitar,' "[12] reveals the procedure by which the imagination creates from the world without reducing it to sterile fixity. The poem opposes mind and flux. The imagination, in the person of a woman, walks beside the perpetually shifting sea (unformed reality) and sings her song. Stevens emphasizes the total separateness of song and sea:

> The sea was not a mask. No more was she.
> The song and water were not medleyed sound
> Even if what she sang was what she heard,
> Since what she sang was uttered word by word.
>
> (CP 128)

The woman's word-by-word utterance matches the mode of the poet: words are the abstractions by which the poet temporarily orders his world into fictive things—poems. In the tradition of Jamesian theory, the woman by the sea engenders reality with her truth. She was "the maker of the song she sang" (CP 129). The observing narrator realizes that although the woman's song is distinct from the sea, it partakes of the sea's motion; by striving to understand the intricacies of the relationship of sea and song— obvious figures for reality and the imagination's rendering of it— the narrator participates in a crucial way in the evolving circumstance. The unraveling drama portrays an allegory of the poetic process, depicting poet, poem, and reader of poem. With the woman as poet and the sea as reality, the narrator as witness becomes a figure for the reader of poems, one who benefits from the poet's formative power and who shares directly in the poet's vision. The narrator recognizes that the woman's words produce an entirely new reality that supersedes either the sea alone or her voice alone. This union produces for the perceiving narrator a vision of wholeness—a profound if momentary experience by which he expands his awareness through the ordering process of the woman's song:

> It was her voice that made
> The sky acutest at its vanishing.

> She measured to the hour its solitude.
> She was the single artificer of the world
> In which she sang. And when she sang, the sea,
> Whatever self it had, became the self
> That was her song, for she was the maker. Then we,
> As we beheld her striding there alone,
> Knew that there never was a world for her
> Except the one she sang and, singing, made.
>
> (CP 129–30)

In "Nature," Emerson proposes that "nature never became a toy to a wise spirit." He continues: "There is a property in the horizon which no man has but he whose eye can integrate all the parts, that is, the poet. . . . The lover of nature is he whose inward and outward senses are still truly adjusted to each other" (CWE I 8–9). The woman at Key West fulfills Emerson's portrait. As "single artificer" whose senses integrate the environment, she—and the imagination for which she is symbol—replaces the deity as the emerging force of the universe. As Emerson's central perceiving poet redeems nature from meaningless plurality by the delicate balance of his perception, so the woman enacts a redeeming visionary song. Like Emerson's scholar, she becomes an active soul whose "insight into to-day" topples the antique and future worlds (CWE I 111). Her world emanates so totally from herself that if she did not utter it, the world could not be. Yet she does not create from nothing. As Edward Kessler remarks, the lady "*discovers* rather than *invents* what she sees. . . . she intensifies what is already there."[13] The process of the sea's "grinding water" and "gasping wind" becomes the process of her melody; man's old distortions of the sea, that it is "ever-hooded" and "tragic-gestured," dissolve in the freshness of her perception. Neither sea nor song submits to fixity since the song changes according to the variations of the naked reality pulsing through it. The creative activity of the woman by the sea substantiates the fundamental Jamesian premise that "the world stands really malleable, waiting to receive its final touches at our hands. . . . it suffers human violence willingly" (PR 456).

The affinity between the creative activity of Stevens' woman by the sea and Emerson's philosophy of genius is particularly strong. In his essay on "Intellect," Emerson announces that "the making a fact the subject of thought raises it" (CWE II 326). This repeats precisely the woman's role: she translates the chaos of nature into a higher form, momentarily ordering it within the mind. Emerson elaborates specifically upon this process and provides a revealing context for explaining the miraculous transposition that occurs in "The Idea of Order at Key West":

The constructive intellect produces thoughts, sentences, poems, plans, designs, systems. It is the generation of the mind, the marriage of thought with nature. To genius must always go two gifts, the thought and the publication. The first is revelation, always a miracle, which no frequency of occurrence or incessant study can ever familiarize. . . . It is the advent of truth into the world, a form of thought now for the first time bursting into the universe . . . a piece of genuine and immeasurable greatness. (CWE II 334–35)

Emerson's genius of mind is Stevens' genius of imagination. Just such a genius, the woman in Key West "sang beyond the genius of the sea" (CP 128). Evolving new forms of thought, her song represents the advent of new truth. Free and unconstrained, the song reflects Emerson's precept that "the thought of genius is spontaneous" (CWE II 336).

In "Owl's Clover," his longest poem and one he excluded from *The Collected Poems,* Stevens searches for the source of the spirit of energy that animates the woman's song in Key West and all creative songs. He concludes that within each man lies a primitive force, a "man below the man below the man, / Steeped in night's opium, evading day" (OP 66). This "subman," as he calls him, embraces imagination and disdains reason; he was "born within us as a second self" (OP 67) and represents a primitive essence who saves man from the "sterile rationalist" with his awful solidifying. The subman is Stevens' drab image for the bare self who sees the flux as it is and can animate it. He is Emerson's scholar, but living in a dungeon, an offspring of Poe's spirit of beauty trapped in a rationalist's world. Stevens ends his sprawling poem with a plea for the release of this subman; he urges sophisticated humanity to submit to primitive force, to the

> passion merely to be
> For the gaudium of being, Jocundus instead
> Of the black-blooded scholar.
>
> (OP 71)

In "The Man with the Blue Guitar" and "Notes Toward a Supreme Fiction," vestiges of the freed subman surface in the guise of the poet-as-hero, Stevens' fullest expression of the central perceiving self.

"The Man with the Blue Guitar" occupies a pivotal position in *The Collected Poems* between the poems of *Ideas of Order* and those of *Parts of a World*; it integrates the discoveries about the nature of imagination and reality that are recurrent themes of both books. More than any poem before "Notes Toward a Supreme Fiction," "Blue Guitar" indicates how far Stevens had progressed since "The Comedian" in his theory that the poet must assume a heroic role in a chaotic universe by ordering his world through imaginative acts. The poet-as-ephebe, who in the person of Crispin staggers through parody and self-directed sarcasm and fails ultimately to assume the responsibilities of Emersonian scholarship, emerges in "Blue Guitar" as one who assertively—even aggressively—accepts a world of process that he alone can articulate. "The Man with the Blue Guitar" posits another aspect of one who, like the lady at Key West, is the "single artificer" of his world, yet without the relative ease of fictive translation the woman enjoys by the calm sea.

A man huddled over his guitar throughout a long, discursive poem recalls not only Picasso's painting, *Old Guitarist*, but Rodin's *Thinker* as well, whose static pose contradicts the emotion and turmoil of mental activity. Each of the poem's thirty-three cantos represents the diverse harmonics of a shifting mind in the act of framing thoughts of a world. The musician struggles with his instrument, experimenting with discordant sounds, toying with what the imagination can do or not do. Each of the poem's cantos might be a single chord, a thought's vibration, which within the stream of consciousness provokes other and disparate vibrations— the process might go on indefinitely. The musical piece that finally evolves displays unity not because of the logical progression from chord to chord, but because the completed work comprises variations on a single theme. Unlike Rodin's, Stevens' thinker plays his imagination upon reality with considerably more than static result. The poem reflects the thinking man's power, of which Emerson wrote in "Circles": "Beware when the great God lets loose a thinker on this planet. Then all things are at risk. It is as when a conflagration has broken out in a great city, and no man knows what is safe, or where it will end" (CWE II 308). Emerson's comment expresses the decreative power of acts of thought, which, by their originality, reduce a world of brittle conceptions to shambles.

"Blue Guitar" creates in poetic form a replica of Emerson's "man thinking," his "central man" who, through imaginative acts, annuls fate and achieves freedom. With Emerson, Stevens' central man could say "I unsettle all things. No facts are to me sacred; none are profane; I simply experiment, an endless seeker with no Past at my back" (CWE II 318). Describing his musician as "A shearsman of sorts" (CP 165), Stevens indicates the guitarist's decreative tendency to "unsettle all things" by trimming reality of the dense foliage of stale fictions. The world out of which the guitarist creates his music is the same demythologized place in which Crispin tried and failed to become a central man:

> There are no shadows in our sun,
>
> Day is desire and night is sleep.
> There are no shadows anywhere.
>
> The earth, for us, is flat and bare.
> There are no shadows.
>
> (CP 167)

Those "silent shadows"—the heavenly spirits and the redemptive Christ—to which the woman in "Sunday Morning" gave her alle-

giance have vanished from the heavens of the guitarist. Acting
upon the starkness of this truth, an audience of common men approaches the guitarist as a replacement-priest of the void. Having
lost the nobility that the existence of God provided them, they
beseech him to ennoble them, to play

> A tune beyond us, yet ourselves,
> A tune upon the blue guitar
> Of things exactly as they are.
>
> (CP 165)

With its poet-audience separation (the duality disappears after
canto vi), the poem becomes a twentieth-century version of "The
American Scholar" address in which a master talks to his students
and illustrates how man can save himself from despair by achieving an original relationship with his universe.

As an emblem of the poet in the modern world, Stevens' guitarist advances Emerson's notion that "the poet is representative.
He stands among partial men for the complete man" (CWE III
5). The audience of disbelievers comes to the guitarist in pursuit
of self-expression. Emerson's belief that "man is only half himself,
the other half is his expression" (CWE III 5) is especially appropriate here since in Stevens' society contemporary man has been
split from his spiritual sources and comes to poetry to discover
wholeness again. Stevens defines the poet's role in clear terms:

> Poetry
>
> Exceeding music must take the place
> Of empty heaven and its hymns,
>
> Ourselves in poetry must take their place.
>
> (CP 167)

Not only does the guitarist express poetry as the supreme fiction
but he enacts what amounts to a religious function as the poet of
the masses. Stevens abandons his notion in "Owl's Clover" that
each man had buried within him a "subman" who, if released,
could become the poet-as-hero. Although the guitarist resembles

the freed subman, Stevens no longer envisions a large community of potential poets. His guitarist, like Emerson's poet, "announces that which no man foretold" (CWE III 8); therefore, he is unique from his audience because, again like Emerson's concept of the true poet, he comes nearer to reality than any other. The poet-self Stevens creates in the image of the guitarist poses an emphatic affirmative reply to James's rhetorical question about the nature of imaginative acts: "Does our act then *create* the world's salvation so far as it makes room for itself, so far as it leaps into the gap" (PR 467)? Leaping into the gap left by the disenfranchised gods, the poet-guitarist creates the world's salvation by means of engendered truths—his own fictions.

Returning to the subject James referred to as "this old dualism of matter and thought" (ERE 185), Stevens' guitarist examines the tenuousness of trying to create new abstractions of the world without changing it. Desiring a tune "beyond us as we are" yet wishing at the same time "nothing changed by the blue guitar" (CP 167), his audience seeks the nearest possible substitute for the kind of permanence-in-impermanence that belief in an afterlife provided. The guitarist cautions that his abstractions can "patch" life but "cannot bring a world quite round" (CP 165) because reality inevitably changes when it filters through the imagination. When the poet tries to "sing a hero's head," when he tries to use his craft as a means of snatching heroism away from the deity and returning it to common man, there must always remain an inevitable separation—"An absence in reality" (CP 176)—between his abstraction of man and man himself; however close the poet's "large eye / And bearded bronze" (CP 165) come to the man, they never can come close enough; the poet captures a heroic version alone, not the real. While admitting the impossibility, the guitarist confesses the desire to "play man number one" (CP 166)—to write the perfect abstraction that would eliminate the distance between reality and poem. The words by which he expresses this wish indicate again the unleashed violence of an imagination at work:

> Ah, but to play man number one,
> To drive the dagger in his heart,
>
> To lay his brain upon the board
> And pick the acrid colors out,
>
> To nail his thought across the door,
> Its wings spread wide to rain and snow,
>
> To strike his living hi and ho,
> To tick it, tock it, turn it true,
>
> To bang it from a savage blue,
> Jangling the metal of the strings.
>
> (CP 166)

Stevens emphasizes in this passage the primitive, forceful nature of the creative act that must ruthlessly subdue the old in order to create the new. In another section, the guitarist says a mind "claws" upon the blue guitar and "its fangs / Articulate its desert days" (CP 174). As in "Farewell to Florida," Stevens again submits to the necessary violence implied in decreation.

In a letter to Hi Simons, Stevens wrote that after *Harmonium* he began to "feel round for a new romanticism." This was because "I began to feel that I was on the edge: that I wanted to get to the center: that I was isolated, and that I wanted to share the common life" (LWS 352). "The Man with the Blue Guitar" implements both his need to get to the center and the need to share the common life. As Riddel observes, Stevens' intention in the poem is "to set the poet, a common self, at the center of the world."[14] Stevens portrays the guitarist in the humble guise of an Emersonian common man, distinguishable solely for his abstracting powers:

> And I am merely a shadow hunched
> Above the arrowy, still strings,
> The maker of a thing yet to be made.
>
> (CP 169)

His heritage encompasses the postwar waste land in which the common man's choices are either to sit "deformed, a naked egg"

and sustain himself on the "cold food" of the old descriptions of
reality, or to "reduce the monster to / Myself" and "be myself /
In face of the monster" (CP 175). He chooses not to follow the
false hero of the twentieth century, the successful corporate ma-
terialist ("pagan in a varnished car" [CP 170]) in whom people
pretend to believe because he represents a final, if hollow, elegance
in a vacuous universe. Rather, like Whitman but with considerably
less reason to sing, the guitarist as the metaphor for the poet commits himself to a processive world that energizes processive songs.
Not only do his fictions become "a dream . . . in which / I can
believe, in face of the object," but as emanations of a fresh commitment of mind to object, the fictions transcend themselves and
form a new reality:

> A dream no longer a dream, a thing,
> Of things as they are, as the blue guitar
> After long strumming on certain nights
> Gives the touch of the senses.

> (CP 174)

At this level, Stevens realized that the poet's fictions achieve the
only finality possible in a flowing and pluralistic universe. Not
final themselves, they can be

> Perceived in a final atmosphere;

> For a moment final, in the way
> The thinking of art seems final when

> The thinking of God is smoky dew.

> (CP 168)

By strumming his guitar, the figure of the poet evolves from
insignificance into a lord in an "immenser heaven" of his own
making:

> A substitute for all the gods:
> This self, not that gold self aloft,

> Alone, one's shadow magnified,
> Lord of the body, looking down,

. . . .
Alone, lord of the land and lord

Of the men that live in the land, high lord.
One's self and the mountains of one's land,

Without shadows, without magnificence,
The flesh, the bone, the dirt, the stone.

(CP 176)

Through the mask of a man strumming a blue guitar, Stevens
voices the discovery upon which his later poetry depends: "Poetry
is the subject of the poem"—not God, nor any other extraneous
matter, but poetry, the process of the mind in the act of making
a world: "From this the poem issues and / To this returns" (CP
176). The man the guitarist evolves—"the old fantoche" wandering through "Oxidia, banal suburb" (CP 181, 182)—stands in the
void of the modern industrial complex and proclaims, "I am"
without despair or loss of freedom. He achieves his central position by confident self-affirmation similar to Whitman's exuberant
song of self:

I am a native in this world
And think in it as a native thinks,

. . . .
Thinking the thoughts I call my own.

(CP 180)

This new poet's creed is one of decreation, requiring that he
"throw away the lights, the definitions" and relinquish "the rotted
names" (CP 183)—the old words that stand between reality and
the poet's idea of reality; his fresh relation to his world enables
him to articulate what he can "see in the dark" and to recognize
"the madness of space" for what it is. For maximum expression,
he must remove all of the old scaffolding that prevents him from
perceiving the world first hand:

Nothing must stand

Between you and the shapes you take
When the crust of shape has been destroyed.

You as you are? You are yourself.
The blue guitar surprises you.

(CP 183)

Stevens expresses through his guitarist what James meant when he wrote that "what really *exists* is not things made but things in the making. Once made, they are dead" (PU 577). "The Man with the Blue Guitar" is a poem "in the making." Each of the mind's fictions expresses a fleeting truth that must dissolve not into fixity but into a new fiction, a fresh surprise from the latest "twang" on the guitar. In James's terms, the guitarist puts himself *"in the making* by a stroke of intuitive sympathy" with the world. The guitarist's strokes are continuous, and James would like that too: "Reality *falls* in passing into conceptual analysis; it *mounts* in living its own undivided life—it buds and bourgeons, changes and creates" (PU 577). In a journal entry, Emerson proposes a blunt variation of James's theory and an appropriate thematic summary for "The Blue Guitar": "Hard blockheads only drive nails all the time; forever remembering; which is fixing. Heroes do not fix but flow, bend forward ever & invent a resource for every moment" (EJ VII 539–40). From the "hard blockhead" who was Crispin, Stevens evolved a poetic hero whose stature expands further toward Stevens' penultimate poem of the self: "Notes Toward a Supreme Fiction."

The central man, or major man as Stevens also refers to him, appears throughout *Parts of a World* testifying to Stevens' sure conviction established in "The Man with the Blue Guitar" that the poet carries out the role of providing the modern era with the fictions by which it can celebrate in a holy vacuum. In "Man and Bottle," the "man at the centre of men" (CP 239) confronts the violence of the universe with an equivalent violence of the mind. Displaying "the fury of a race of men," the poet at the center creates poems that lash "more fiercely than the wind," destroying "romantic tenements" in order to find what will suffice. In "Of Modern Poetry," the central man appears as "an insatiable actor" who, like a misplaced Hamlet, struts upon the stage of a theater wholly different from Shakespeare's time, since his world, once out of joint, can never be restored to order. An obvious extension of Stevens' guitarist, the actor also recognizes poetry as the only subject of poems; his "twanging" justifies his existence:

> The actor is
> A metaphysician in the dark, twanging
> An instrument, twanging a wiry string that gives
> Sounds passing through sudden rightnesses, wholly
> Containing the mind, below which it cannot descend,
> Beyond which it has no will to rise.
>
> (CP 240)

In the programmatic "Examination of the Hero in a Time of War," Stevens investigates at great length the lineaments of the hero and concludes that "There is no image of the hero," that all references to him must be destroyed because "this actor / Is anonymous and cannot help it" (CP 278–79). Since the hero "is not a person" (CP 276) and has no image, he seems a composite of Emersonian selfhood:

> The highest man with nothing higher
> Than himself, his self, the self that embraces
> The self of the hero, the solar single.
>
> (CP 280)

"The search after the great man," says Emerson in his collection of essays "Representative Men," "is the dream of youth and the most serious occupation of manhood" (CWE IV 3). For Stevens, the search for the central man evolves into a recognition that he is an abstraction for the common man and that he possesses qualities that each man possesses. As Susan Weston observes, "this central man is nothing but us—an 'idea of man'. . . . this hero is an 'identity' for the thing of the imagination."[15] Weston takes the discussion another crucial step. She notices that Stevens frequently associates the figure of the hero with language and speaking, which helps to explain the significance that Stevens imparts to the hero-symbol: "the birth of the hero becomes a way of articulating the interaction between world as chaos and world as word. Just as important, the hero becomes a kind of bridge between the silent self and the undeciphered world. The articulation of the one is the definition of the other."[16] As a "kind of bridge" between self and world, the hero conforms to a parallel function that Stevens outlines for the poet in "The Noble Rider and the Sound of Words." Recognizing that poetry "is not a social obligation" and that the poet cannot "lead people out of the confusion in which they find themselves," Stevens asserts nevertheless that the poet links people to himself in the same vital way in which the guitarist was linked to his audience: "I think that his function is to make his imagination theirs" Stevens writes, "and that he fulfills himself only as he sees his imagination become the light in the minds of others. His role, in short, is to help people to live their lives" (NA 28–29). This clearly advances Emerson, who wrote: "The poet . . . has a whole new experience to unfold; he will tell us how it was with him, and all men will be the richer in his fortune. . . . the world seems always waiting for its poet" (CWE III 10). The role of the poet and the role of the hero fuse for Stevens. The poetic self produces through the force of imaginative perception "a violence from within that protects us from a violence without" (NA 36); by acts of decreative violence, the poet experiences temporary apotheosis and replaces the deity as the creative center of existence.

"Notes Toward a Supreme Fiction" climaxes the evolution of the Emersonian scholar-ephebe, or young poet. Stevens' poetic voice emerges in "Notes" to the maturity of one who understands the complexities of a pluralistic universe and embraces enthusiastically the role of poet-maker in a nonteleological world. The poem expresses an aesthetic coalescence, which, by the very fact of its being composed, announces fresh directions.

In the poem's opening section, Stevens sets forth the familiar teacher-student motif: "Begin, ephebe, by perceiving the idea / Of this invention, this invented world" (CP 380). In other poems using the educational framework—"Sunday Morning" and "A High-Toned Old Christian Woman," for instance—the separation between professor and scholar is obvious, but in "Notes" the narrator could easily be addressing tandem extremes within himself.

As both ephebe and poet, he has progressed significantly in the ways of his craft and must now submit himself to an extensive review and application of what he has learned. In this mundane sense, Stevens' "Notes" represents the last in a series of aesthetic lessons to the student in himself who has matriculated from inchling to "prodigious scholar" (CP 381) and now reviews the procedure by which he came to that crucial stage in his poetic life that allows him to stand confidently at the hub of his world. In the first of the three major divisions of the piece, "It Must Be Abstract," the separation between narrator and ephebe remains complete, but in "It Must Change" and "It Must Give Pleasure," teacher and student dissolve into one another and emerge a first-person narrator, a proclaiming "I" and integrated self whose voice comes as close to Stevens' own as any of the voices in his poems. The ephebe-as-student of division one merges into the ephebe-as-poet in divisions two and three and participates directly in writing the poem that climaxes his growth.

Although Stevens frequently referred to the poem as "a collection of just what I have called it: Notes" (LWS 443), he recognized its pivotal position in his canon. In 1946, four years after completing it, he requested that the publisher of *Transport to Summer* begin the poem on a separate page because it was "the most important thing in the book" (LWS 538). Stamped with Stevens' sense of its importance and containing so much of what critics have discovered as vintage Stevens, it is little wonder that "Notes" has been critically discussed at much length.

In a letter to Gilbert Montague in 1943, Stevens indicates his awareness that "Notes" was written in the bias of William James:

Underlying ["Notes"] is the idea that, in the various predicaments of belief, it might be possible to yield, or to try to yield, ourselves to a declared fiction.

This is the same thing as saying that it might be possible for us to believe in something that we know to be untrue. Of course, we do that every day, but we don't make the most of the fact that we do it out of the need to believe, what in your day, and mine, in Cambridge was called the will to believe. (LWS 443)

This direct allusion to James's famous essay, "The Will to Believe," establishes a major source for Stevens' theory of fictions. James proposes his essay as "a defence of our right to adopt a believing attitude in religious matters" (WB 717). He argues that since "no concrete test of what is really true has ever been agreed upon," the empiricist must abandon the doctrine of objective certitude and admit that "we find no proposition ever regarded by any one as evidently certain that has not either been called a falsehood, or at least had its truth sincerely questioned" (WB 725). When James acknowledges that "biologically considered, our minds are as ready to grind out falsehood as veracity" (WB 727), he anticipates Stevens' contention that "it might be possible for us to believe in something that we know to be untrue." Since objective truth cannot be proven, James exhorts the empiricist to live "by the practical faith that we must go on experiencing and thinking over our experience, for only thus can our opinions grow more true" (WB 725). Denying what he calls the schoolboy's definition of faith as belief in "something that you know ain't true," he affirms nevertheless that "we have the right to believe at our own risk any hypothesis that is live enough to tempt our will" (WB 733–34). He concludes that the single "indefectibly certain truth" is that "the present phenomenon of consciousness exists" (WB 725). Beyond that, certitude is not possible.

Clearly, Stevens' passing reference to James's essay on "The Will to Believe" indicates at least an indirect influence of the famous essay on the particular theses of "Notes" and on his themes in general. In James's statements rests the essence of Stevens' theory that poetry is the supreme fiction. For Stevens, the imagination satisfies man's need to believe by continuously forming "hypotheses" of reality "live enough" for the mind to consider. These hypotheses are fictions—figures of imaginative structuring—that originate from a desire to approach as close to reality as possible. Since both mind and world are in a state of constant flux, the fictions perpetually change. In James's phrase, they emanate from the process of man "experiencing and thinking over" his experience. Direct parallels to "Notes" are obvious: because reality changes, the poet's fictive creations of reality "must change"; because the poet abstracts from reality and expresses his fictions in words, then his fictions "must be abstract"; and because existence, in its "vast repetitions" (CP 405) and in the beauty of its particulars, is pleasurable, then his fictions "must give pleasure." Once he assumes a position as the sole arbiter of his reality by denying the old hypotheses and creating his own, the ephebe-poet graduates to the "man-hero" (CP 406). He replaces the defunct gods who were not the supreme creators of the universe after all: "The death of one god is the death of all" (CP 381). Through what Stevens calls "the more than rational distortion, / The fiction that results from feeling" (CP 406), the poet creates a new invention of the world and, by each creative act, he participates in the only form of supremacy a processive existence allows. In place of the supreme truths of the absolutist, he substitutes the supreme fictions of the poet-empiricist and he discovers in his ability to create fresh ideas of the world the "majesty" he thought belonged to deity:

> There is a month, a year, there is a time
> In which majesty is a mirror of the self:
> I have not but I am and as I am, I am.
>
> (CP 405)

In total self-definition, the poet endorses cyclical change and postulates a philosophy of freedom and the peace of knowing in the nonteleological world that the "merely going round is a final good" (CP 405).

Another facet of the rich complexity of "Notes" brings forward James's notion that "language works against our perception of the truth" (PP 34). Stevens' poem investigates the tyranny of language and the paradox of the poet, who must perceive the world originally without locking it into the stale concepts language breeds. "Words," writes James, "uttered or unexpressed, are the handiest mental elements we have. Not only are they very *rapidly* revivable, but they are revivable as actual sensations more easily than any other items of our experience" (PP 54). As poet, Stevens of course concurs with the importance of words, yet he rejects the tendency of man to freeze reality into verbal conceptions. In "It Must Be Abstract," Stevens advises the ephebe that he

> must become an ignorant man again
> And see the sun again with an ignorant eye
> And see it clearly in the idea of it.

(CP 380)

In short, the ephebe must strip the conceptualized sun of its verbal myths so that the language by which man describes it does not inhibit him from perceiving it originally. "Phoebus is dead" because "Phoebus was / A name for something that never could be named" (CP 381).

By relinquishing verbal categories, the poet attains a glimpse of what Stevens refers to as the "first idea," a revelation of the primitive source of mind and reality alike: "The poem refreshes life so that we share, / For a moment, the first idea" (CP 382). Poems invigorate existence by bringing both poet and reader to a point of "ever-early candor," from which the first idea—reality without preconception—may be perceived. But man moves between two points. The opposing point to candor is "its late plural," which denotes the categories, systems, and so on added after initial insight. Stevens conceives of the "first idea" as essentially foreign to man—"a muddy centre before we breathed. / . . . a myth before the myth began" (CP 383). In this time before man's time, there was a wholeness, a completeness; striving to attain the wholeness of that center, the poet writes poems:

> From this the poem springs: that we live in a place
> That is not our own and, much more, not ourselves
> And hard it is in spite of blazoned days.

(CP 383)

Stevens' notion of the "first idea" repeats James's notion of pure experience. James does not subscribe to a theory of a time pre-existent to man that man strives to reach; he projects instead an "instant field of the present" when experience is unmodified by language and is just "plain, unqualified actuality, or existence, a simple *that*" (ERE 177–78). Experience at this level precedes experience as a state of mind and, therefore, "in its passing is always 'truth,' practical truth, *something to act on*, at its own movement" (ERE 178). Like Stevens' "first idea," James's "instant field of the present" involves an aspect of the primitive; it is a generative source from which everything proceeds and to which everything returns. James describes it as

> this present actuality with which things confront us, from which all our theoretical constructions are derived and to which they must all return and be linked under penalty of floating in the air and in the unreal; this actuality, I say, is homogeneous—nay, more than homogeneous, but numerically one—with a certain part of our inner life.
>
> (ERE 168)

Stevens conceives the "first idea" "not our own," yet, like James, he sees it as elemental truth, which the poet by creating poems strives to achieve. The "ravishments of truth," however, are "so fatal to / The truth itself" that the "first idea" is lost—"becomes / The hermit in a poet's metaphors" (CP 381). As the poet's single means of embodying the first idea, paradoxically, language inhibits his attempts to do so. To avoid the tyranny of words, the poet's challenge requires that he attain the moment of "ever-early candor," which originates not from thought but from feeling, or, more precisely, from "thought / Beating in the heart" (CP 382). Having attained this condition, although the poet's poems will still be abstractions of reality—"False flick, false form"—yet, they will be as "An abstraction blooded, as a man by thought" (CP 385). Their falseness will be "falseness close to kin," (CP 385) which will bring the poet as near to a vision of the first idea as it is possible for him to come: "As if the language suddenly, with ease, / Said things it had laboriously spoken" (CP 387).

Stevens' three major themes in "Notes Toward a Supreme Fiction" evolve out of this notion that the poet's abstractions must originate from the *feeling* that comes from original perception—

from seeing "with an ignorant eye" (CP 380). If they originate from mere thoughts, they are abstractions simply, not "abstraction[s] blooded," and they partake not of the "early candor" but of the conceptual rigidity of the "late plural" where first ideas harden into fixity. They must not be fictions simply, but "the fiction that results from feeling," and feeling results not from conception but from perception of naked reality. Again, James provides the clarifying insight: "Our sensations," he writes, "are not small inner duplicates of things, they are the things themselves in so far as the things are presented to us" (ERE 186). Man comes closest to naked reality through the dynamism of perceiving his world without the benefit of man's conceptions of it. "These percepts," James concludes, "these *termini*, these sensible things, these mere matters-of-acquaintance, are the only realities we ever directly know and the whole history of our thought is the history of our substitution of one of them for another, and the reduction of the substitute to the status of a conceptual sign" (MT 151). The urgency of Stevens, Emerson, and James alike to position themselves at the center of their world is here explained. Only at the center, where sensation is the same as bare reality, can true pleasure and authentic change reside, and there alone can the poet assure himself that his abstractions are "blooded." James's insistence on the vitality of sensations that flow from original perception directly coincides to the advice that Stevens extends to the ephebe in "Notes." James even uses the "Rock," precisely the same figure Stevens uses as an image for the naked center of reality:

Contemned though they be by some thinkers, these sensations are the mother-earth, the anchorage, the stable rock, the first and last limits, the *terminus a quo* and the *terminus ad quem* of the mind. To find such sensational *termini* should be our aim with all our higher thought. They end discussion; they destroy the false conceit of knowledge; and without them we are all at sea with each other's meaning. (MT 151)

The parallel of Stevens' rock to James's is so striking that it goes beyond mere affinity of consciousness. In "Credences of Summer"

Stevens will say "The rock cannot be broken. It is the truth" (CP 375). And in "The Rock," the title poem of his last book, he will refer to it in several ways:

> The rock is the gray particular of man's life,
> The stone from which he rises. . . .
>
> . . . .
>
> The rock is the stern particular of the air,
> The mirror of the planets, one by one,
>
> . . . .
>
> The rock is the habitation of the whole,
> Its strength and measure, . . .
>
> . . . .
>
> The starting point of the human and the end.
>
> (CP 528)

For Stevens and James both, the rock is the *terminus a quo* and *terminus ad quem* of the mind. The source of this major image in Stevens' poetry is William James.

Canto vii of "It Must Be Abstract" summarizes the empirical kind of "truth" that the poet attains when, by means of the sudden balances that nature provides, he transcends the artificiality of man's categories and experiences what James calls "sensational termini"—that intensity of feeling that accompanies "flicks" of fictive vision:

> It feels good as it is without the giant,
> A thinker of the first idea. Perhaps
> The truth depends on a walk around a lake,
>
> A composing as the body tires, a stop
> To see hepatica, a stop to watch
> A definition growing certain and
>
> A wait within that certainty, a rest
> In the swags of pine-trees bordering the lake.
> Perhaps there are times of inherent excellence,
>
> As when the cock crows on the left and all
> Is well, incalculable balances,
> At which a kind of Swiss perfection comes

And a familiar music of the machine
Sets up its Schwärmerei, not balances
That we achieve but balances that happen,

As a man and woman meet and love forthwith.
Perhaps there are moments of awakening,
Extreme, fortuitous, personal, in which

We more than awaken, sit on the edge of sleep,
As on an elevation, and behold
The academies like structures in a mist.

(CP 386)

Having delineated the nature of abstraction, the narrator of "Notes" shifts his lesson to Stevens' old subject—the poet-hero in whom rests the power to create the "abstraction blooded." The gradual emergence of the ephebe throughout the entire canon climaxes in the last three cantos of "It Must Be Abstract," in which Stevens painstakingly meditates the relationship of poem to maker of poems. But the poet-hero he settles upon, both as an abstraction toward which the ephebe should aspire and as a figure for the central man, deemphasizes the figure of the major man that Stevens had been developing in the poems before "Notes." Stevens subdues his notion of heroism and returns to the common man in a processive world as the appropriate figure for the poet— a combining into single form Emerson's "Poet" and "American Scholar."

In "The Man with the Blue Guitar," the guitarist, as a figure for the poet, voices the essential attribute of Stevens' hero: "I sing a hero's head, large eye / And bearded bronze, but not a man" (CP 165). Despite the particularity in which Stevens dresses him in several poems, the hero partakes of man but remains beyond man; he is an abstraction, enigmatic, and, except in sudden "flicks," as elusive as the "first idea." Stevens repeatedly describes him in images of transparence, a word both Emerson and Shelley had used to mean visions. In "Asides on the Oboe," the hero is "the human globe," "the transparence of the place," "the man of glass, / Who in a million diamonds sums us up" (CP 250–51); in

"Notes," he is a "crystal hypothesis" (CP 387), an "inanimate, difficult visage" (CP 388). These figures advance Emerson's famous vision of himself as a solitary man in intense communion with nature: "Standing on the bare ground,—my head bathed by the blithe air and uplifted into infinite space,—all mean egotism vanishes. I become a transparent eyeball; I am nothing; I see all; the currents of the Universal Being circulate through me. . . . I am the lover of uncontained and immortal beauty" (CWE I 10).

In "Notes," Stevens initially portrays the major man as he had previously: "an imagined thing," an emanation from a common man "MacCullough" who, like Emerson's central man, "lay lounging by the sea" (CP 387) in intense communion with nature. Through acts of the imagination, MacCullough absorbs the world into himself, abandons the rigid preconceptions of the "late plural" and attains the moment of original insight, the point of "ever-early candor"; then, in abstract language so powerful that it was "As if the waves at last were never broken" (CP 387), he voices his experience. Through the natural process of "man thinking" and then uttering, MacCullough joins himself to the world of fresh occurrence and defines the proper interrelation of self with world and world with self. The narrator establishes the vital point that, despite the clairvoyance of MacCullough's "romantic intoning" (CP 387), he is, after all, a real man, not an apotheosis: "MacCullough is MacCullough" (CP 387). Then Stevens enacts a curious parable depicting the birth of the major man in the specific imagery of Christ's nativity. The language signifies that the major man is about to be canonized a replacement savior of the common man. He comes "Lighted at midnight," and "Swaddled in revery" (CP 388), he "reposes / On a breast forever precious"—the breast of a maternal "dame" who combines, perhaps, the antique roles of muse and virgin and of whom the narrator requests to "sing for this person [the infant major man] accurate songs" (CP 388). Stevens intends here not a parody of the Christ myth so much as a nativity-parallel of sufficient magnitude to underscore the major man's significance. His parable of the Christ-fiction is itself a fiction through which he indicates that in a world without teleology, man's salvation depends upon himself. The major man as a fictive replacement for the obsolete Christ emanates not from God but from the mind of man.

Having created another powerful symbol of the major man, Stevens alters the importance he ascribed to him in his other poems of the hero. He advises the ephebe to "give him / No names" and to "dismiss him from your images" (CP 388). Clearly, Stevens realizes that the figure of the major man, like the myth of Christ, was becoming too much of a fixity in his canon and belonged on the dump with other worn-out figures. By dismissing the major man's images, Stevens avoids the error of the various heroes in "It Must Change"—men like General DuPuy, Canon Aspirin and Ozymandias who, in abortive attempts to create enduring fictions, create foolish statues instead. Reducing the significance of one of the principal figures in his poems, Stevens takes still another step in the evolution of himself as a central perceiving poet. The deemphasis represents his choice to preserve the idea of the major man but not to be preoccupied with the idea.

In the final section of "It Must Be Abstract," Stevens introduces a new hero to replace his old figure. He is one of "these separate figures" (CP 389) of common mankind whom rabbis and chieftains see every day passing under their leadership. He is "part, / Though an heroic part, of the commonal" (CP 388). Compared to the inflated figure of the major man, he is a dumpish clown

> in his old coat,
> His slouching pantaloons, beyond the town,
> Looking for what was, where it used to be.
>
> (CP 389)

The ephebe must learn that he is of this man and of the real world. He must assume the humble guise of the men of whom he writes. Like Emerson's "Poet," he "must pass for a fool and a churl for a long season" (CWE III 41) and know that the major man is a minor man in tattered coat, a "vagabond in metaphor" (CP 397)—an image for the world. "Since he is a cumulative figure," William Burney writes, "through him one can look at oneself. By constantly rubbing that glass clear of past associations, the ideal poet can ensure ever-fresh receptions of first ideas and, having all the time in the world, make poems of them."[17] The imagination must continually interpenetrate with the vagabond's world if it is to fulfill its function of creating abstractions blooded by feeling:

> It is he. The man
> In that old coat, those sagging pantaloons,
>
> It is of him, ephebe, to make, to confect
> The final elegance, not to console
> Nor sanctify, but plainly to propound.

(CP 389)

Having learned this lesson, Stevens' ephebe acquires his maturest voice, which, in "It Must Change" and "It Must Give Pleasure," merges with Stevens' own voice and produces fictions appropriate to a poet at the center of a pluralistic universe. The hesitation that typifies the poetic voices in Stevens' earlier poems dissolves into the confident affirmations of a speaker witnessing the process of his own fiction-making. The poet-speaker of "Notes" reconstitutes Emerson's portrait of "the rich poets," who "resemble a mirror carried through the street, ready to render an image of every created thing" (CWE III 41). More clearly than ever, Stevens' narrator realizes the nature of the changing world, the origin of that change, and the function of the poem to move "from the poet's gibberish to / The gibberish of the vulgate and back again" (CP 396). With Emerson and James, he subscribes to "inconstant objects of inconstant cause / In a universe of inconstancy"; he postulates that "the distaste we feel for this withered scene / Is that it has not changed enough" (CP 389-90).

As a central perceiving self, the ephebe-poet discovers that the supreme fiction means simply "to find the real," to watch it come "from its crude compoundings"—the old imposed fictions in which it suffocates—and then to see it like "a beast disgorged" and "stripped of every fiction except one"—the one in which the poet himself discovers it and clothes it by his imaginative act, the one that is the "fiction of an absolute" (CP 404)—his own poem. The constant repetition of this process renders the poet him "that of repetition is most master" (CP 406). The "Mere repetitions" (CP 405) of the constantly changing world become the poet's paradise, a far better place than the mythy heaven where angels sing: "I can / Do all that angels can" (CP 405). Released from the demands of a nonearthly paradise, the poet's fictive song becomes its own end—"A thing final in itself and, therefore, good." (CP 405).

In the closing lines of "Notes," Stevens bestows upon his ephebe-poet the function of naming the universe. No longer a "beast disgorged," reality stripped of its sterile myths becomes the feminine principle the poet seeks—his "Fat girl, terrestrial, my summer, my night" (CP 406). Emerson's concept of the poet as "sayer" and "namer" and as the "sovereign" who "stands on the centre" (CWE III 7) is realized in the closing couplet as Stevens' ephebe invokes his imaginative power to name his world: "I call you by name, my green, my fluent mundo. / You will have stopped revolving except in crystal" (CP 407).

By dividing his "grand poem," as some refer to it, into elaborations on three imperative statements, Stevens invites—perhaps intentionally—misinterpretation. He intends the imperatives as essential qualifications that a fiction must fulfill in order that it may be called "supreme": "It Must Be Abstract," "It Must Change," and "It Must Give Pleasure." Such categorical imperatives contradict an empirical philosophy of the universe based on the notion of process, and certainly, by their rigid emphasis, they contradict all Stevens had discovered as an emerging self in a pluralistic world. What might be fitting signs tacked above Crispin's cabin door in the Carolinas have no place in a poem celebrating change and urging a commitment to an inconstant yet holy universe. "Notes Toward a Supreme Fiction" carries a residue of the imperative and of dogma that extends beyond the "musts" into the notion of supremacy itself. Somewhat like Crispin, yet in a far less severe fashion, it seems that Stevens intends "Notes" as a program for the mind's activities in which the poet-hero—Stevens himself—can arbitrate the flux and can become, in Stevens' own words from "The Noble Rider," "the light in the minds of others" (NA 29).

The long poems that follow "Notes" indicate that Stevens may have realized that he came close in this poem to committing his own unpardonable sin—imposing a system on process. "The greatest empiricists among us," James reminds, "are only empiricists on reflection; when left to their instincts, they dogmatize like infallible popes" (WB 724). After "Notes," Stevens discards the notion of the hero as well as the tripartite system for achieving supreme fictions. The late poems avoid emphatic statements concerning what the mind can, should, or must do and become instead exquisite illustrations of the process of doing it.

3 TRANSPORT TO SUMMER

Antiteleology as Source of
Freedom and Hope

tevens completed "Notes Toward a Supreme Fiction" in 1942. After carefully delineating the ingredients comprising supreme fictions, he attached a revealing epilogue to the poem, which indicates his uneasiness that, while he had been constructing a notion of poetry as the supreme relevance in man's experience, the bombardments of World War II were devastating Europe. His "Notes" had not taken these evils into account and his sensitivity to this prompted a coda by which he could plant himself as poet into the international arena of dying soldiers and political atrocities:

> Soldier, there is a war between the mind
> And sky, between thought and day and night. It is
> For that the poet is always in the sun.

> (CP 407)

Stevens' apostrophe to the soldier borders on apology. He assures him that the poet's war with reality parallels his war, that in fact, "the two are one." As if trying to justify the imperative coming in the height of the conflict, that poetry "must give pleasure," Stevens contends that whereas the soldier's war ends, the poet's war continues since, as part of the imagination's unceasing struggle with reality, the poet must embody the soldier's exploits in his "petty syllabi," or poems. By translating reality into "sounds that stick, / Inevitably modulating, in the blood," the poet creates an identity for the soldier that he otherwise would not possess: "Monsieur and comrade, / The soldier is poor without the poet's lines" (CP 407). The poet enriches the soldier's significance by abstracting his heroism and suffering; in turn, the poet's involvement in matters of war assures his social integrity since "war for war, each has its gallant kind" (CP 407).

Helen Hennessy Vendler is right in referring to the coda as "Stevens' most notorious attempt to prove that poetry and life are interdependent."[1] In "Notes" Stevens assimilated his poetic creed into a formal aesthetic, which he offered to society as a means for interpreting and resolving significant social issues of the day.[2] The epilogue attempts to justify the program Stevens articulated in the poem itself. It represents an effort, on the one hand, to reconcile life-lived with his aesthetic theory; at the same time, employed as an addendum, it reveals his intuition that his fixed idea of supremacy was not a panacea for social atrocities. This strained effort to yoke the war of the world and the war of poetry into "a plural, a right and left, a pair" (CP 407) becomes, by the urgency of its assertion, an admission that the project had failed. Stevens realized that "Notes Toward a Supreme Fiction" performed no social function whatsoever, that its imperatives were hollow in the context of the war and dying. In the poems written after "Notes," he renounces the notion of a supreme poetry simply by never again referring to it. He withdraws his aesthetic theories from the public rostrum and returns to his earlier private investigation of the processes by which mind and reality interrelate.

But if he renounced his notion of supremacy, he could not renounce the war. The details of the conflict brought Stevens to a realization of evil far surpassing the abstract and metaphysical notions of pain and suffering that had been a real part of his "mind of winter" as far back as *Harmonium*. Insofar as it acted as a major influence on the procedures in the later poems in his canon, the effect of the war on Stevens directly parallels the impact social calamities had on the lives of Emerson and James. There came critical times for both of them when the actions of their government and their countrymen outweighed their own poetical and intellectual activities to such a degree that they were forced to stop and adjust their philosophies. As Stevens would, they discovered man-generated evil to be worse than any metaphysical, philosophical, or theological conceptions they had of it. Absorbing the ramifications of this discovery into their respective philosophies required a personal expansion of views already liberal yet not elastic enough to admit such harsh realities without internal growth.

In Emerson's case, the Mexican and Civil wars rattled his idealism and threatened his philosophical roots since both conflicts, especially the latter, involved attacks on the integrity of the human personality, which Emerson so staunchly defended. Until the 1840s, and especially in the 1850s, Emerson was not much distracted by political issues. But by the time of the passing of the Fugitive Slave Law in 1850, his journals more and more are filled with the issues of slavery and the impending war. He wrote two long essays on the Slave Law itself as well as an essay on the state of American civilization under the shadow of slavery. In addition to these, he delivered numerous speeches on such varied topics as John Brown, the Emancipation Proclamation and the death of Lincoln. In the 1840s, he predicted America's war with Mexico "will poison us" (EJ IX 430–31), called patriotism "balderdash," and discovered America a "Lilliput," its countrymen "free willers, fussy, self asserting, buzzing all round creation" (EJ X 30). American imperialism and greed dampen the dream of a country of scholarly selves. In his essay "War," he tried to diminish war's significance by conceiving it as an inevitable plateau in the advance of civilizations.

War, which to sane men at the present day begins to look like an epidemic insanity, breaking out here and there like the cholera or influenza, infecting men's brains instead of their bowels,—when seen in the remote past, in the infancy of society, appears a part of the connection of events, and, in its place, necessary. (CWE XI 151)

But he wrote this ten years before the Civil War started and he was unable to sustain theoretical rationalization in the context of concrete violence. By 1862, his conclusions were more empirical and subdued. "War," he wrote, "is a realist, shatters everything

flimsy & shifty, sets aside all false issues, & breaks through all that
is not as real as itself" (EJ XV 299). By this time too, the war
had become for him "this blot . . . this heavy load," a "malaria
which the purest winds and strongest sunshine could not penetrate and purge." So preoccupied and outraged was he by 1864
that he concluded the Civil War had established a new calendar
for America: "The cannon will not suffer any other sound to be
heard for miles and for years around it. Our chronology has lost
all old distinctions in one date,—*Before the War, and Since*" (EJ
XV 300).

The Civil War and the slavery issue focused for Emerson the
extremes of human degradation and forced him to reevaluate the
significance of evil and fate to his philosophy. The concepts of
evil and of tragedy are weak notions in Emerson's early philosophy
because his theory of compensation implied the individual's power
to vanquish fate by strength of character. The young Emerson did
not possess Stevens' "mind of winter." He did not recognize, as
Stevens had, the extent of man's finitude. In spite of Emerson's
many attacks on Christianity and on the divine person of Jesus,
his notion of evil issued nevertheless from an orthodox Christian
base. Redemption took care of evil for him so that it did not
become a strain to his imagination or to his thinking. He wrote:
"To him who by God's grace has seen that by being a mere tun-
nel or pipe through which the divine Will flows, he becomes
great, & becomes a Man,—the future wears an eternal smile &
the flight of time is no longer dreadful. I assure myself always of
needed help, & go to the grave undaunted because I go not to the
grave" (EJ V 96). As he explored the potential of the individual
to act out his own destiny, evil became less and less a significant
issue. Since tragedy contributed to character, it could hardly be
called tragedy at all. An 1838 journal entry illustrates his tendency
to minimize the impact of the tragic on his life:

I told J[ones]. V[ery]. that I had never suffered, & that I could scarce
bring myself to feel a concern for the safety & life of my nearest friends
that would satisfy them: that I saw clearly that if my wife, my child,
my mother, should be taken from me, I should still remain whole with

the same capacity of cheap enjoyment from all things. I should not grieve enough, although I love them. But could I make them feel what I feel—the boundless resources of the soul,—remaining entire when particular threads of relation are snapped,—I should then dismiss forever the little remains of uneasiness I have in regard to them. (EJ VII 132)

Stephen Whicher contends that the price of Emerson's experiment in self-reliance was to deny the tragic sense of life to his philosophy. "With Melville, we like men who dive," Whicher writes, "but not when they come up to report that deep water is an illusion."[3]

As Emerson matured, he relinquished the idealism of an unlimited self with "boundless resources." The disillusion and skepticism that appear in the later journals and essays came gradually and in the specific context of Emerson's increasing involvement in a pluralistic America where transcendence seemed less and less a possibility. He acknowledged to a larger degree the tremendous power of nature and qualified many of the blatant assertions of his early optimism. In "Experience," for example, he admits, "I am not the novice I was fourteen, nor even seven years ago" (CWE III 83). The later essays concern a world of facticity, and if his philosophy does not become a radical empiricism, it becomes empirical enough for F. I. Carpenter's tag, "pragmatic transcendentalism," to be accurate. Metamorphosis, the essential ingredient of the universe for Emerson, began to weigh upon him. "I take this evanescence and lubricity of all objects, which lets them slip through our fingers then when we clutch hardest, to be the most unhandsome part of our condition" (CWE III 49). Within the context of his own aging, cyclical process and necessity posed concrete threats. To Caroline Sturgis Tappan in 1853, he wrote: "Friends are few, thoughts are few, facts few—only one; one only fact, now tragically, now tenderly, now exultingly illustrated in sky, in earth, in men & women, Fate, Fate" (LE IV 376). Emerson's disillusion culminated as the Mexican War ended and the slavery issue was propelling America toward civil war. Man-made catastrophe served as the catalyst through which Emerson arrived at a point of balance between skepticism and freedom. "Great men," he concluded in his essay "Fate," "have not been boasters and buffoons, but perceivers of the terror of life, and have manned themselves to face it" (CWE VI 5). The older Emerson, sensitive to his own youthful excursions into boasting and idealistic buffoonery, recognized that "Nature is no sentimentalist," that the world is "rough and surly, and will not mind drowning a man or a woman" (CWE VI 6). Written between two wars, "Fate" expands Emerson's philosophy beyond what Whicher calls the "rhapsodic songs" of "Nature." The Emerson who wrote "The American Scholar" would not have noticed what he acknowledged in "Fate"—that "famine, typhus, frost, war, suicide and effete races must be reckoned calculable parts of the system of the world" (CWE VI 19). Neither would the essayist of "Self-Reliance" have been able to enter into his journal, as Emerson did in 1850, a statement acquiescing to his sense of futility: "The badness of the times is making death attractive" (EJ XI 250).

    Characteristically, Emerson recovered from the internal antagonism his confrontation with literal evil brought to him. His belief in the "Power" of the individual compels him to conclude "Fate" with a call to "build altars to the Beautiful Necessity" because she enables man to realize the fullness of his powers and thus "plants the rose of beauty on the brow of chaos" (CWE VI 48). His choice to embrace the natural and chaotic world after painfully absorbing the implications of Fate and man-made evil relates him directly to Wallace Stevens, as analysis of Stevens' poem "Esthétique du Mal" will indicate.

    For William James, on the other hand, evil is not absolved by orthodox commitment to Christ and the redemptive act. James could not so easily evade the issue as the young Emerson had done. Monism created the problem of how imperfection can issue from a perfect source; but with pluralism, James contends, evil "presents only the practical problem of how to get rid of it" (SPP 268). James's empiricism states that evil is known solely in terms of this world and this environment. Nothing transempirical need enter into it. By reducing the issue of evil to the practical level, pragmatism frees man's mind from the necessity of solving

a metaphysical problem and places him squarely in the physical
world. James states his position emphatically:

the words 'good,' 'bad,' and 'obligation' . . . mean no absolute natures, independent of personal support. They are objects of feeling and
desire, which have no foothold or anchorage in Being, apart from the
existence of actually living minds.
    Wherever such minds exist, with judgments of good and ill, and
demands upon one another, there is an ethical world in its essential
features. Were all other things, gods and men and starry heavens,
blotted out from this universe, and were there left but one rock with
two loving souls upon it, that rock would have as thoroughly moral a
constitution as any possible world which the eternities and immensities
could harbor. . . .
    We, on this terrestrial globe, so far as the visible facts go, are just
like the inhabitants of such a rock. Whether a God exist, or whether
no God exist, . . . we form at any rate an ethical republic here below.
(WB 618–19)

Once again, we see James using the image of the rock, the precise
image Stevens uses as a figure for the essential center of the universe. The image of two people on a rock personifies Stevens' notion in "Notes" of returning to the point of the "first idea." James
removes evil from any philosophical or theological contexts and
forces man to partake of the luxury of his actual world—his rock
of existence. By preoccupying himself with abstract diversity and
abstract evil, man loses his grasp on the physical universe. "Divinity lies all about us," he writes, "and culture is too hide-bound to
even suspect the fact" (TT 650). This is precisely the narrator's
point in "Sunday Morning" when he admonishes the Christian
woman that "Divinity must live within herself" (CP 67). James
scorns the charm and hollow peace that transempirical systems
such as Christianity provide:

This human drama without a villain or a pang; this community so
refined that ice-cream soda-water is the utmost offering it can make
to the brute animal in man; . . . this atrocious harmlessness of all
things,—I cannot abide with them. Let me take my chances again in
the big outside worldly wilderness with all its sins and sufferings. (TT
647)

For James, as for Emerson, the "outside worldly wilderness" comprised at times an enormity of man-made evil to which he had to make continual adjustments. Again, war became a significant catalyst, which so outraged James that assimilating it, however necessary, was difficult. His disgust with America's entrance into war with Spain in 1898 equalled the disturbance the Mexican and Civil wars caused Emerson. He saw the conflict as a repulsive example of "barbaric patriotism" in which America had nothing to gain but satisfaction of its "passion for adventure." "We are in so little danger from Spain," he wrote to Theodore Flournoy, "that our interest in the war can only be called that in a peculiarly exciting kind of *sport*."[4] The bitterness of James's satire illustrates that, despite his willingness to take his chances, the harshness of the world was a continual threat to him. His biting comments to Flournoy expressed severe disillusion with humanity's violent primal instincts:

And after all hasn't the spirit of the life of all the great generals and rulers & aristocracies always been the spirit of sport carried to its supreme expression? Civilization, properly so called, might well be termed the organization of all those functions that resist the mere excitement of sport. But *excitements!*—shall we not worship excitement?—It makes all humdrum moralizing seem terribly dead and tame![5]

But even this does not express the extent of his exasperation. He reserved his most vituperous comments on the war for a letter sent to the *Boston Evening Transcript* in 1899:

The individual lives are nothing. Our duty and our destiny call, and civilization must go on! Could there be a more damning indictment of that whole bloated idol termed "modern civilization" than this amounts to? Civilization is, then, the big, hollow, resounding, corrupting, sophisticating, confusing torrent of mere brutal momentum and irrationality that brings forth fruits like this.[6]

Unlike Emerson, James had no need to coordinate man's malignancy to orthodox premises. "In any pluralistic metaphysic," he writes, "the problems that evil presents are practical, not speculative. Not why evil should exist at all, but how we can lessen the actual amount of it, is the sole question we need there consider" (PU 526-27). If the maleficence of war made the practical question of lessening the amount of evil seem irresolvable, James insisted nevertheless that answers must be sought in unidealized daily life, not in orthodox systems and hollow speculative reasoning. "The more we live by our intellect," he quotes Tolstoï in an essay entitled "What Makes a Life Significant," "the less we understand the meaning of life. We see only a cruel jest in suffering and death" (TT 651). Eschewing empty speculation, James counseled instead the absorption of evil into the processes of daily living since a "delightful and sinful" world is the only reality we know and therefore the only base upon which an empirical philosophy can be founded:

Sweat and effort, human nature strained to its uttermost and on the rack, yet getting through alive, and then turning its back on its success to pursue another more rare and arduous still—this is the sort of thing the presence of which inspires us, and the reality of which it seems to be the function of all the higher forms of literature and fine art to bring home to us and suggest. (TT 648)

James urges the acceptance of pain and evil as inevitable aspects of processive living, the only fit subject of art.

Wallace Stevens, like Emerson and James, faced in World War II man-generated evil worse than any he had conceived possible. Like them, he did not recoil from it but, by deliberate assimilation, converted pain and suffering into aspects of process within the empirical world. In "Esthétique du Mal," Stevens moved from understanding evil as a phenomenon of a philosophical or theological system to conceiving it as an empirical fact within the physical world. He moved therefore from the orthodox thinking of Emerson to the empiricist thinking of William James. This was the major adjustment of his later poetry. By relieving his mind of the last vestige of metaphysical, theological, or philosophical system, Stevens freed the imagination to a world in which it can redeem reality by its own generative visions.

As the coda to "Notes" suggests, World War II brought to

Stevens a vivid if grim reminder of man's inhumanity to man. For the most part, he deliberately avoided specific comment about the war. In 1944, when a prose commentary on "War and Poetry" was requested of him, he replied that such a commentary from him was "out of the question," then continued: "I wonder if the war has not ceased to affect us except as a part of necessity, as something that must be carried on and finished, with no end to the sacrifice involved. But I think that even the men in the Army etc. feel that it is no longer anything except an overwhelming grind" (LWS 479). Earlier comments reveal however that the war affected him deeply. Writing to Leonard C. van Geyzel in 1939, he confessed that "as the news of the development of the war comes in, I feel a horror of it: a horror of the fact that such a thing could occur" (LWS 342). To Henry Church in 1940, he expressed sensitivity to the paradox of a preoccupation with poetry in an atmosphere of war. "The climate is changing," he wrote, "and it seems pretty clearly to be becoming less and less a climate of literature" (LWS 365). Near the end of the conflict, in 1945, this paradox surfaced more emphatically in another letter to Mr. Geyzel: "At the moment, the war is shifting from Europe to Asia, and why one should be writing about poetry at all is hard to understand" (LWS 501). To James Guthrie in the same year, he expressed "an impression of profound disturbance and of bewilderment as to the [war's] outcome, and of intense doubt as to the purposes of the disturbance." The same letter contains a comment reminiscent of the bitterness of Emerson and James to nineteenth-century wars: "What all this means is a general change in our ideas respecting other people. I don't think that most of us have realized the extent to which conspiracy and greed and gall dominate the world" (LWS 507).

Stevens' outrage should not imply that he had ever evaded—as Emerson had—the problem of evil. His "mind of winter" issued from an awareness that the beauty in existence depends upon death and disorder. As Daniel Fuchs notes, evil for Stevens primarily means "metaphysical evil, which," Fuchs says, "includes the realities of death, pain, unseemliness, and the many other limitations of finite, imperfect existence."[7] He adds, however, that there is a "social meaning to the word," and this is the context in which Stevens uses it in "Esthétique du Mal." The relentless literal—or "social"—minutiae of the war diluted the confidence of the central perceiving self that Stevens developed to its most emphatic voice in "Notes."

The difficulties Stevens had of accomplishing this surface in the poems of war that serve as preludes to "Esthétique." In "Dutch Graves in Bucks County," written in 1943, Stevens returned to the graveyard of his maternal ancestors and tried to discover between the dead past and violent present a continuity sufficient to sustain the imagination in a time of war. The eerie setting coupled with the vivid details of battle generate a tone suitable to the subject. In the quiet cemetery, the imagination fills the night with a din of unheard sounds that attach the "Angry men and furious machines" of World War II to the religious conflict of the poet's Dutch "semblables" who, in the "sooty residence" of their vaults, "Tap skeleton drums inaudibly" (CP 290). Although past and present fuse in the imagination's eye, the speaker realizes that in the absoluteness of death, his ancestors "Know that the past is not part of the present" (CP 291). Death as "a profounder logic" brings an end to the incoherent evil, but every age must realize the logic for itself. Each generation searches a "new glory of new men" (CP 292) no matter what lessons the past might offer to them. The imagination consoles itself with the knowledge that the "stale perfections" of "archaic freedom"—the freedom ancestors thought they were winning for their children—cannot sustain vibrant living in a chaotic present. One grim reality of process requires accepting that within the birth-death cycle, the "mobs of birth" seek out their own perfections, "waiting until we go / To picnic in the ruins that we leave" (CP 293).

In "Dutch Graves," Stevens took a significant step toward assuaging his outrage over the war. Since man lives in process and evil is man-made, then man's wars for freedom are the inevitable

expression of cyclical recurrence. The violence of good confronting evil occurs regardless of history's influence. Freedom is always
to be won violently:

> Freedom is like a man who kills himself
> Each night, an incessant butcher, whose knife
> Grows sharp in blood. The armies kill themselves,
> And in their blood an ancient evil dies—
> The action of incorrigible tragedy.
>
> (CP 292)

Though the "violent marchers" of every age enact their contest in
the face of inevitable annihilation, their energies are essential
nevertheless because within cyclical patterning their march is
"toward a generation's centre" (CP 293). A curious paradox in
"Dutch Graves" is that, while Stevens denies the influence of the
past on the present, clearly affirming their separation, he joins
them by his imaginative structuring. He blends the struggle and
pain of his forebears into his present dilemma. While history defines no inherent links of age to age, the poem indicates that
imagination can discover its own essential relationships.

In "No Possum, No Sop, No Taters," which was written in the
same year as "Dutch Graves" and immediately follows it in *The
Collected Poems*, Stevens expresses—this time without directly
mentioning the war—the difficulty of imaginative activity in a
context of the war's somber reality. Similar to the early *Harmonium* piece, "The Snow Man," "No Possum" concerns a win-
tertime when the mind is most in danger of annihilation: "The
field is frozen. The leaves are dry. / Bad is final in this light" (CP
293). The imagination perceives reality in the figures of World
War II's mutilation:

> In this bleak air the broken stalks
> Have arms without hands. They have trunks
>
> Without legs or, for that, without heads.
> They have heads in which a captive cry
>
> Is merely the moving of a tongue.
>
> (CP 293-94)

As in "The Snow Man," where the imagination learned to distinguish between the "Nothing that is not there and the nothing that is" (CP 10), in "No Possum" Stevens learned that by absorbing the savagery of evil into the imagination's life, he could locate hope in the atmosphere of despair: "It is here, in this bad, that we reach / The last purity of the knowledge of good" (CP 294). A crow with "malice in his eye," evil preserves the imagination from sterility in winter's void by enervating fresh contemplations of reality: "One joins him there for company, / But at a distance, in another tree" (CP 294). In bleak winter, evil provides a form of solace because it constitutes a form of life.

In "Repetitions of a Young Captain," published in the spring of 1944, a few months before "Esthétique Du Mal" first appeared in *The Kenyon Review*, Stevens continued to examine the jarring impact of war upon himself and his generation. As James Baird points out, "every young captain in every war rests in this speaker. Hence, he signifies the endless repetition of violence in the human condition which we call war."[8] Through his belabored repetitions, the captain tries to reconstruct for his imagination the place he occupied before the "tempest cracked on the theatre" and the war shattered, psychologically as well as physically, what "had been real" but "was not now" (CP 306).[9] Fitting together pieces of the self that he was to the self that he is, the captain struggles to achieve psychic equilibrium. Forced to be one soldier among "Millions of major men against their like" (CP 307), he witnessed in the war a destruction-creation process; now, an appropriate emblem of modern man living in "a calculated chaos," he stands amid ruin in "an external world" and discovers "the spectacle of a new reality" (CP 306). His way is difficult because the war has destroyed every structure by means of which he previously defined his identity. Stevens uses the war motif in this poem to restate the assumptions of his entire aesthetic—that the old protective theater of the gods is gone, the props destroyed; man must issue from the shadows of the tenements of the past and renew his relationship to a naked reality. From the rubble of war, the captain emerges a private self, one of "The powdered personals against the giants' rage" (CP 309). He discovers a new reality "beyond / The finikin spectres in the memory" (CP 307). In the tradition of the Emerson-James man, he has regained the actual world and must learn now to live in it.

In these poems of war, Stevens acclimates his imagination to the extremity of pain and suffering that man himself generates. They open the way to the major discussion of pain and evil in "Esthétique." On June 17, Stevens wrote the following note to John Crowe Ransom, responding to a recent issue of *The Kenyon Review*:

What particularly interested me was the letter from one of your correspondents about the relation between poetry and what he called pain. Whatever he may mean, it may be interesting to try to do an esthetique du mal. It is the kind of idea that it is difficult to shake off. Perhaps that would be my subject in one form or another. (LWS 468)

Stevens was ready to tackle all of the subtleties of a problem "Notes" had completely ignored. By doing so, he thrust his poetry toward its major phase.

Helen Hennessy Vendler finds the fifteen cantos of "Esthétique du Mal" "violently unconnected in tone" and considers the poem "at once the most random and the most pretentious of Stevens' long poems." With "Description Without Place," she labels "Esthétique" an "experimental" poem that "seem[s] in fact to be a regression after the self-confident finish of 'Notes'."[10] Vendler misses the point that if the poem regresses at all, it does so in the positive sense that Stevens realized that, for the self-confidence in "Notes" to be legitimate, he had to expand, much as Emerson and James did, his notion of *mal*. Expansion requires backtracking. The fifteen cantos represent fifteen variations on the theme of evil and pain, both of which are implied in the translation of the French noun, *mal*. If Stevens' old themes appear under a new heading, the reasons for the repetitions are organic and expansive, not regressive. By terming Stevens' effort to link evil and aesthetics "pretentious," Vendler blithely casts aside the relevance of the poem to the rest of Stevens' canon. Certainly, Daniel Fuchs is more accurate in finding "Esthétique" "one of the masterpieces" of Stevens' later work.[11]

Stevens locates the intrinsic center of the poem in the very first stanza. A male protagonist—an aged version of the ephebe-scholar of "Notes" as well as an obvious figure for Stevens himself—sits in Naples intermittently writing letters and reading "paragraphs / On the sublime" (CP 313). The groanings of the Vesuvius volcano recall to him the ancient phrases by which imaginative men of the past had expressed their terror of the sound. "He tried to remember the phrases: pain / Audible at noon, pain torturing itself" (CP 314). In the midst of these recollections, which by their inflated language partake of the mood of the sublime, the man experiences hunger pangs; he casually returns to human mundanities and realizes, almost as an afterthought, the essential truth about pain and suffering:

> It was almost time for lunch. Pain is human.
> There were roses in the cool café. His book
> Made sure of the most correct catastrophe.
> Except for us, Vesuvius might consume
> In solid fire the utmost earth and know
> No pain (ignoring the cocks that crow us up
> To die). This is a part of the sublime
> From which we shrink. And yet, except for us,
> The total past felt nothing when destroyed.
>
> (CP 314)

As Stevens had said in "Dutch Graves in Bucks County," past and present combine only through imaginative intervention. Now he extends the point another step. The sublime notions of pain in myth and literature are nothing but the fictive creations of past imaginations. The irony of Stevens' quick shift from the mythic rumblings of pain within the intestines of Vesuvius to the man's hunger reduces the sublime to the human and equates, with humorous subtlety, the voracious appetite of the earth feeding upon itself to the appetite of a humble man sitting in a cool cafe awaiting lunch. (Stevens uses the appetite metaphor again in canto vi in the image of sun and world insatiably feeding upon each other.) The man's letters and the book's rendition of "the most correct catastrophe" emphasize further that man conjures his own emotional interpretations of the universe. Without man and outside of time (which in the image of crowing cocks is but another of man's projections), sublime reasons for the paradox of evil and pain could not exist. We "shrink" from this notion of the sublime because we require a transempirical security by which to make pain endurable. Daniel Fuchs provides an important insight here: "if a deity is the cause of sublimity in nature, our aesthetic indulgence receives a sanction it does not achieve when one experiences sublimity on purely secular grounds. Unmotivated by a wish to indulge in deist notions, one finds violence more mysterious, vastness more terrifying."[12]

By acknowledging that "pain is human," that it is a function of life-lived, Stevens frees evil from the interpretations of philosophy and theology and places it within the limits of processive reality. He thus accomplishes his most dramatic shift from orthodoxy to empiricism, from Emerson to James. In the remaining fourteen cantos of "Esthétique du Mal," Stevens examines the systems of belief from which the concepts of pain and evil must be freed and proposes, finally, the single possible conclusion to which his analysis brings him.

In canto ii, which Fuchs labels Stevens' "dark night of the soul," the protagonist investigates personal causes for projecting a transempirical source for pain and evil. Lying upon a balcony at night, he notices that the particulars of his world comprise acacias and warbling birds, the transitory natures of which elicit from him the severe melancholy whose throne Keats had discovered to be with "beauty that must die." To escape the despair of the awareness of dying that beauty communicates, he transfers his attention to the rising moon. In this instance, the moon is not Stevens' familiar figure for the imagination. Because it was "a supremacy always / Above him" and "was always free from him" (CP 314), the moon becomes a figure for the consolation man provides for himself by inventing spiritual and poetic systems of belief. But now the protagonist realizes that pain "is indifferent to the sky" and has nothing to do with the hallucinations of supremacy his desire for peace has prompted him to find there.

Having dismissed the false solace that imaginative projections of supremacy provide, in canto iii the protagonist becomes the modern poet whose "firm stanzas hang like hives in hell" (CP 315). He recognizes that "now both heaven and hell / Are one," which is to say that imperfections and perfection, evil and good, ugliness and beauty, are not extraneous to but contained within the dynamism of the activity we call life. The "firm" base of his fictions provides a forum from which the poet analyzes the impact of Christianity upon man's notion of evil:

> The fault lies with an over-human god,
> Who by sympathy has made himself a man
>
> . . . .
>
> A too, too human god, self-pity's kin
> And uncourageous genesis.

(CP 315)

By becoming human, Christ robbed man of his rightful experience of pain. He pitied man too much and, by the redemptive act, cured man of the imperfections he inherited from Adam's fall. Instead of leaving redemption in the hands of man, the Christian myth "Weaken[s] our fate" by relieving us of woe, which, as a natural function of living, should be a source not of weakness but of strength. The too human god, or Christ, is "self-pity's kin" because he is the imaginative creation of men who so pitied themselves at having to suffer pain and death that they fashioned an elaborate spiritual system by which to free themselves from their natural yoke. Stevens affirms that man does not need these "uncourageous" modifications of evil. By releasing pain from "satanic mimicry," man can regain the strength the redemptive myth sapped from him and will enjoy living more fully in his world:

> It seems
> As if the health of the world might be enough.
>
> It seems as if the honey of common summer
> Might be enough. . . .

> As if pain, no longer satanic mimicry,
> Could be borne, as if we were sure to find our way.
>
>   (CP 315–16)

In a much more radical way, Stevens' rejection of Christ restates Emerson's struggle with Christianity as it surfaced most
dramatically in "The Divinity School Address." Emerson com-
plains that the name of Jesus "is not so much written as ploughed
into the history of this world" (CWE I 126). He laments that
man distorts the Christian myth, converts it to a "Monster" that
"is not one with the blowing clover and the falling rain" (CWE
I 129). Yet Emerson rejects not the myth, but man's distortions
of it. He disparages the "noxious exaggeration about the *person*
of Jesus" (CWE I 130) and, while adhering to an orthodox base,
calls for man to spurn lifeless rigidity and to return to a religion
of resilience: "One would rather be 'A pagan, suckled in a creed
outworn,' than to be defrauded of his manly right in coming into
nature and finding not names and places, not land and professions, but even virtue and truth foreclosed and monopolized"
(CWE I 131).

In canto iv, Stevens denies a sentimentalist approach to nature
and pain. The sentimentalist groups "All sorts of flowers" under
a single abstraction. By generalizing the world, he ignores its
facticity, which is its essence. Opposed to the sentimentalist is
the "genius of misfortune," one for whom "fault / Falls out on
everything" (CP 316). His course must be rejected because while
embracing evil he denies the good. He represents the nihilist of
the modern era. In place of either extreme, Stevens proposes "that
Spaniard of the rose," an image of a poet who particularizes
reality, sees evil for what it is, and achieves the proper balance
between the mind's conceptions and the world's facts. As a manifestation of this balance, canto v returns emphatically to the
empirical world and illustrates the newly achieved bliss that
emanates from man's rejection of the metaphysical systems of
evil. Stevens summons "all true sympathizers" to come "Without
the inventions of sorrow" and to share "Within the actual . . . /

So great a unity, that it is bliss" (CP 317). The sympathizers discover the joy and experience the love of being wholly human, not
sponsored by any theology or myth. They return to the condition
of the primitive "Before we . . . knew ourselves," when good and
evil were natural aspects of the "nebulous brilliancies" of living.
They reexperience a "central sense" in which "these minutiae" of
their exquisite factual world "mean more / Than clouds, benevo-
lences, distant heads" (CP 317). The sympathizers comprise a
world of central people who replace the promise of eternity with a
bliss more deeply felt because it issues from their imperfect selves.

Fuchs refers to canto vi as "a somewhat forced attempt at displaying the imperfections of nature."[13] What Stevens is actually
doing is retelling in parable form the evolution of a processive
world. In the image of a comic Prometheus, the sun "in clownish
yellow" carries fire into the world. Striving to bring each day to perfection, the sun is doomed to failure because cosmic time depends
on his interrelationship with "the lunar month." Moon-night
follows day-sun perpetually. Space is filled with the "Rejected
years" (past time) of the sun's abortive quests for perfection.
Meanwhile, "a big bird pecks at him / For food" (CP 318).
If the sun is a comic figure of Prometheus, then the bird, who
"Rose from an imperfection of its own," may be a comic Satan.
But if the sun is a figure for itself, then the bird is the world,
which feeds unsatiably upon the sun's energy. Stevens echoes by
exaggeration the appetite of the man in the cafe whose hunger is
the final extension of the evolving process of bird feeding upon
sun. The "grossest appetite" of the sun's fire "becomes less gross"
in the context of earth's appetite for energy and the interdependence of bird and sun produce what Emerson refers to as the perpetual inchoation of existence. Stevens' parable portrays evolution
in terms of imperfection and pain. The unquenchable appetites
of opposing energies, much like the forces of imagination and
reality, produce the vibrancy that is the nature of change.

In canto vii, Stevens inverts his emphasis from cosmic motion
to human pain and assimilates once and for all the meaning of
evil and suffering inherent in war:

> How red the rose that is the soldier's wound,
> The wounds of many soldiers, the wounds of all
> The soldiers that have fallen, red in blood,
> The soldier of time grown deathless in great size.
>
> (CP 318–19)

The soldier is a common man whose heroism derives from the intensity by which he lived his life. "His wound is good because life was" (CP 319). Since the wound is part of the process of life, it is good. By extension, since war is part of the same process, it must be good too, at least in the sense that it produces the communal death scene Stevens describes. The living share the wounds of their dead, so all mankind, by their nature, wears the soldier's rose, which combines beauty and pain.

Stevens relieves the serious tone of canto vii by presenting in canto viii a humorous parable of the fall of Satan. In this version, Satan's defeat surprised even him because it did not follow a mythic struggle with the gods. Instead, "a capital / Negation destroyed him in his tenement" (CP 319). By saying no to Satan and to the stale fictions comprising him, man stimulates "the imagination's new beginning" (CP 320). Even so, "The death of Satan was a tragedy / For the imagination" because it eliminated man's most powerful symbol for the cause of pain. To fill the void of Satan's exit, the imagination turns to a reality it had never before witnessed except in the context of the myth of evil spirits:

> How cold the vacancy
> When the phantoms are gone and the shaken realist
> First sees reality.
>
> (CP 320)

The tragedy of the death of Satan causes fresh imaginative visions that are based upon the notion of evil not as a divine but as a human paradox.

Canto ix studies "the shaken realist" of canto viii in greater depth by returning to the night balcony scene of canto ii in which the poet contemplates the moon's relationship to pain. The dismissal of the old structures of belief produces "Panic in the face of the moon" (CP 320) because the moon no longer harbors the fictions through which man viewed it: "nothing is left but comic ugliness / Or a lustred nothingness" (CP 320). With the sky divested of its system, man stands naked in a decreated universe. In one of his strongest statements of nonteleological hope, Stevens calls for "Another chant, an incantation" that will be the music of a new order of poets responding to "a primitive ecstasy" of the universe. Through central songs emanating from what Stevens called in "Notes" the "first idea," man conquers panic and "drowns the crickets' sound" (CP 321). The next canto expresses yet another positive embrace of a life of change and evil after the disappearance of "the nostalgias" of old beliefs. Attaching himself to the "sleek ensolacings" by which the old fictions provided peace, man prevented the experience of the barrenness of reality and the simplicity of pain. The old nostalgias sequestered pain in fantastic parables. By embracing the world's fertile center, Stevens finds "reality explained" and discovers death and pain unencumbered by myth as natural occurrences: "That he might suffer or that / He might die was the innocence of living" (CP 322).

Canto xi provides violent contrast to the consolations of the previous canto. While indicating the necessity of recognizing that "pain is human," Stevens refuses to moderate it. He underlines the grim disparity between paratroopers falling from the skies in Europe and American suburbanites apathetically mowing their lawns. Joseph Riddel interprets the statement "Life is a bitter aspic. We are not / At the centre of a diamond" (CP 322) as an indication that "Emerson's central man . . . has been displaced at the center of things."[14] But Stevens emphasizes not displacement so much as acceptance of the bitterness that the central position implies. Continuing the imagery of hunger that threads through the poem, he portrays "A man of bitter appetite," a poet who, while despising society's efforts to sidestep evil by confecting it in flowery, contrived language, must at the same time feed upon "these exacerbations . . . / Like hunger that feeds on its own hungriness" (CP 323). The poet supplies the "essential savor" of evil's true import and shares his nutrients with the world. An epicure of "The gaiety of language," his words provide man the only redemption that can be his now that the redemptive myths have evaporated. Stevens embodies his thesis in a deceptively playful couplet that indicates the power of words to rescue man from his forlorn condition: "Natives of poverty, children of malheur, / The gaiety of language is our seigneur" (CP 322).

After delineating the proper place of language in the world of "malheur," in cantos xii and xiv Stevens disparages the false rationalism by which man uses language to disperse the world into precise categories. Besides separating man from intimate contact with his environment, the tyranny of reason over imagination leads to the formation of emotive causes and ideologies. Stevens employs a sample from Russian politics to illustrate that "revolution / Is the affair of logical lunatics" (CP 324). Because reason replaces facticity with abstraction, those who pursue intellectual structures merely "promenade amid the grandeurs of the mind." William James had established that "rationalism is always monistic" (PR 365). With James's monists, Stevens' "lunatic of one idea" denies pluralism and subjects people to "Live, write, suffer and die in that idea / In a world of ideas" (CP 325). Rational lunatics reject James's pragmatic rule that requires that abstracts and universals lead back into sensible experience before they can lay claim upon truth or falsity. Since the politics of emotion evades the particular world, the revolutionists' "extreme of logic" is illogical. Stevens portrays the evil of evading a pluralistic universe as far more serious than any of the evils comprising such a universe.

Appropriately, after a protracted examination of evil, "Esthétique du Mal" climaxes with a profound affirmation of life in an empirical universe:

> The greatest poverty is not to live
> In a physical world, to feel that one's desire
> Is too difficult to tell from despair.
>
> (CP 325)

Seeking the vagueness of an unreachable paradise, man easily confuses his spiritual desires with the despair of being unable to satisfy them. Of all man's poverties—and "Esthétique" accumulates a considerable list—the greatest is to miss "The green corn gleaming," to replace the richness of particularity with the hollow promise of a nonphysical heaven. If man embraces pain and evil as portions of his human lot, he can expel obsolete spiritual systems, and earth will be his paradise regained. "This is the thesis scrivened in delight, / The reverberating psalm, the right chorale" (CP 326). As Fuchs notices, the language here possesses a biblical quality, which "lends a sanctity to Stevens' secular enterprise."[15] The naked world Stevens inherits by purging his mind of the metaphysical systems of evil is holier than the paradise the Christian myth proposes. Stevens' poem celebrates the delight of empirical existence and closes with an expression of the joy of living in a holy and secular universe:

> And out of what one sees and hears and out
> Of what one feels, who could have thought to make
> So many selves, so many sensuous worlds,
> As if the air, the mid-day air, was swarming
> With the metaphysical changes that occur,
> Merely in living as and where we live.
>
> (CP 326)

Through moments of imaginative insight, moments of seeing, hearing, feeling, man repeatedly discovers a plural reality that, within the tenuous relationship of evil to good, is quite enough to sustain him.

The discoveries in "Esthétique du Mal," by purging the mind of spiritual structures, enable Stevens to begin redeeming nature through the medium of his own visions, a process he initiates in "Credences of Summer." Commitment to a visionary world is also a pivotal phenomenon in the writings of Emerson and James. Stevens' mystic visions derive from both of them. For all three writers, visionary moments are personal religious experiences, although in James's and Stevens' case, not in any orthodox sense. In *The Varieties of Religious Experience*, James characterizes these experiences at some length. He claims that "personal religion," since it does not, like the established Church, depend upon "second-hand" traditions, is "more fundamental than either theology or ecclesiasticism" (VRE 31).[16] He defines religion as *the feelings, acts, and experiences of individual men in their solitude, so far as they apprehend themselves to stand in relation to whatever they may consider the divine*" (VRE 31–32). James concludes that when understood in this context, "a man's religion might thus be identified with his attitude, whatever it might be, toward what he felt to be the primal truth" (VRE 35). "The divine" comes to mean "only such a primal reality as the individual feels impelled to respond to solemnly and gravely, and neither by a curse nor a jest" (VRE 39). As an analysis of "Credences" will show, the secular aesthetic at which Stevens arrives by denouncing orthodox theory in "Esthétique du Mal" comprises, under the criteria established by William James, "religious" experience of a "divine" essence. For Stevens, the divine consists in visionary moments of intense illumination when the mind penetrates through stale morphology to the generative and creative center of existence. These visions constitute vital and brief perceptions of wholeness that challenge the imagination to create fresh images of what it has witnessed. Each poem then represents a partial glimpse or "flick" of the energizing center of both mind and world.

James depicts such visionary moments in precise terms. He realizes that, in the ordinary sequence of life's flow, moments endlessly pass into later moments that interpret and correct the former. Opposed to these, however, are "living moments" that involve "something entirely unparalleled by anything in verbal thought." Seeming to "well up from out of their very centre," each of these instants "stands and contains and sums up all things; and all change is within it. . . ." James concludes this passage by declaring that "something as paradoxical as this lies in every present moment of life." Then follows a specific reference to Emerson: "Here or nowhere, as Emerson says, is the whole fact."[17]

James's allusion to Emerson signifies that a tradition subscribing to "living moments" extends from Emerson and Whitman through

James to Stevens. Emerson noticed that "there is a difference between one and another hour of life in their authority and subsequent effect" (CWE II 267). He saw that faith comes in "brief moments" that constrain us "to ascribe more reality to them than to all other experiences." Man is forced to acknowledge that "from some alien energy the visions come" of a "pure nature" that language cannot paint because it is "too subtle . . . undefinable . . . but we know that it pervades and contains us" (CWE II 268–71). One such vision for Emerson was the episode in "Nature" that resulted in the famed "transparent eyeball" passage. From standing on bare ground, he is suddenly "uplifted into infinite space" and "the currents of the Universal Being circulate through me" (CWE I 10). Nature becomes a fitting setting for such moments to occur. In the same paragraph Emerson records another visionary instant: "Crossing a bare common, in snow puddles, at twilight, under a clouded sky, without having in my thoughts any occurrence of special good fortune, I have enjoyed a perfect exhilaration. I am glad to the brink of fear" (CWE I 9). In his essay "The Over-Soul," Emerson describes such instants as the abandonment of self to "the Supreme Mind." The language he uses to describe one's sentiment in this state resembles the figures Stevens uses to detail similar events in his poetry. Emerson writes:

In ascending to this primary and aboriginal sentiment we have come from our remote station on the circumference instantaneously to the centre of the world, where, as in the closet of God, we see causes, and anticipate the universe, which is but a slow effect. (CWE II 276)

This compares to Stevens' imagery in "The Ultimate Poem Is Abstract":

> It would be enough
> If we were ever, just once, at the middle, fixed
> In This Beautiful World Of Ours and not as now,
>
> Helplessly at the edge, enough to be
> Complete, because at the middle, if only in sense
> And in that enormous sense, merely enjoy.
>
> (CP 430)

The major difference between Emerson's visions and those in
Stevens' late poetry is that whereas Stevens' originate within his
own imagination, are self-generative and creative, Emerson's originate out of an orthodox framework, are extrapersonal and non-
creative. Stevens' result from imaginative *action in* the world,
Emerson's from imaginative *openness to* the world. The vision's
sources differ, but their qualities are the same.   '

In his essay "Mysticism," James avers that "personal religious
experience has its root and centre in mystical states of consciousness" (VRE 370). Since Stevens' visions subscribe to James's
definition of a religious experience, they may be referred to as
mystical states. James confirms, as Emerson had, that a frequent
context for the evocation of mystical states is nature: "certain aspects of nature seem to have a peculiar power of awakening . . .
mystical moods" (VRE 385). Among his examples illustrating
nature's power are one from Amiel's *Journal in Time* and another
from Walt Whitman's *Leaves of Grass*. Amiel refers to various
instances of being in nature—at sunrise, on a mountain top, at the
foot of a tree—in which one experiences "moments divine, ecstatic
hours . . . instants of irresistible intuition in which one feels
one's self great as the universe, and calm as a god. . . . The vestiges they leave behind are enough to fill us with belief and enthusiasm" (VRE 386). From Whitman, James cites as a "classical
expression" of the "sporadic type of mystical experience" this
famous passage:

> I mind how once we lay, such a transparent summer
>   morning.
> Swiftly arose and spread around me the peace and
>   knowledge that pass all the argument of the earth,
> And I know that the hand of God is the promise of my own,
> And I know that the spirit of God is the brother of
>   my own,
> And that all the men ever born are also my brothers
>   and the women my sisters and lovers. . . .
>   (VRE 387)

These examples of mystical moments occurring within the

splendor of nature relate directly to "Credences of Summer," in which Stevens records, in the highly charged language of a holy event, a vision of major import. So sacred is this incident that an effective means of interpreting it is through the four qualities that William James delineates as the common "marks" of mystical experience. The first of these is Ineffability. Inevitably, James affirms, one who attains a mystical experience declares that it "defies expression," that "no adequate report of its contents can be given in words" (VRE 371). The second is Noetic Quality. To those who achieve them, mystical states are states of knowledge; "they are illuminations, revelations, full of significance and importance, all inarticulate though they remain; and as a rule they carry with them a curious sense of authority for aftertime" (VRE 371). The third, Transiency. A mystical state can be sustained for only short periods of time. The fourth, Passivity. When the state has set in, "the mystic feels as if his own will were in abeyance, and indeed sometimes as if he were grasped and held by a superior power" (VRE 372). Although these qualities cannot be rigidly imposed upon "Credences," they provide a helpful means for discovering a difficult poem.

The relationship between "Esthétique du Mal" and "Credences" clarifies the details of Stevens' vision. His struggles with evil yielded the optimistic conclusion that not to live in a physical world was the only evil man need fear. Yet, by advocating a total embrace of nature's process, Stevens realizes that as nature comes to full life in summer, then dies in winter, the imagination, if it adheres to seasonal patterns, must follow a parallel cycle of fruition and exhaustion. The vision that results in "Credences of Summer" indicates that Stevens had found a way to separate the imagination from the "downward to darkness" (CP 70) pattern of nature's cycles without simultaneously separating himself from the joys of life's process. "Credences" ventures to describe the essential factors of this vision. Its success must be limited because, as Stevens recognizes in "Description Without Place," description is never "The thing described" but always "an artificial thing" (CP 344). The vision is bound to remain unexpressed, yet Stevens does what he can to capture its flavor. Thus, the insight that culminates in "Credences" conforms to the first of James's qualities for the mystical state—that it defy expression. Stevens uses several parables to try to illustrate that he had found a new time scheme for the imagination's life, that the imagination could be free from dependence on nature's patterns and could replace them with patterns of its own. In the midsummer splendor of nature's ripeness, Stevens experiences a mystical moment similar to Whitman's and Amiel's, in which he learns that the words of poetry carry redemptive power. As emanations of the imagination's visions, they save man from the violence of reality's cycles by creating fictions through which the imagination disengages itself from reality's endless birth-death patterns and creates instead an internal sequence of its own.

The first section of "Credences," the most important of the poem, satisfies the Jamesian "marks" for the mystical state:

> Now in midsummer come and all fools slaughtered
> And spring's infuriations over and a long way
> To the first autumnal inhalations, young broods
> Are in the grass, the roses are heavy with a weight
> Of fragrance and the mind lays by its trouble.
>
> Now the mind lays by its trouble and considers.
> The fidgets of remembrance come to this.
> This is the last day of a certain year
> Beyond which there is nothing left of time.
> It comes to this and the imagination's life.

(CP 372)

In summer's ripeness, in the lull between spring's ascendence and autumn's decline, the imagination "lays by its trouble" and basks in contemplative passivity. In this state the mind, like summer, is ripe for submission to what James called a "superior power," which turns out to be the lushness of the present moment in the instant of nature's consummate expression. The double emphasis on "now" not only indicates Stevens' intense concentration on the visionary moment, but also forbodes his awareness of the transiency of the state and anticipates attempts in the later stanzas to recapture in fictive parables what in the first three stanzas comes as close as Stevens ever comes to capturing the actual scene of his contemplation. The echoing "nows" suggest still other meanings that establish "Credences" as a pivotal poem in Stevens' canon. The chronology of events leading up to the publication of "Credences" in 1947 prompts one to postulate that Stevens meant: now that the war is over, now after I have composed an aesthetic of evil, now in the sixty-eighth year of the imagination's life, and now within a lull in the sequences of my career—*now* I have realized a theory of poetry that can be a theory of life, and I shall write about it. Acting upon his confidence in this vision, he dismantles history and calendars, makes this midsummer day the last within the old structure of marking time, and generates an entirely new system for the imagination's life. He fulfills then James's noetic quality requiring that a mystical state include revelations "full of significance and importance" and that they carry with them "a curious sense of authority for after time" (VRE 371).

The calculated restraint by which Stevens expresses his discoveries in canto i dissolves into strident, celebrational imperatives in the second canto:

> Postpone the anatomy of summer, as
> The physical pine, the metaphysical pine.
> Let's see the very thing and nothing else.
> Let's see it with the hottest fire of sight.
> Burn everything not part of it to ash.

(CP 373)

The gusto of these lines recalls a similar mood in the famous funeral poem, "The Emperor of Ice-Cream": "Let be be finale of seem. / . . . Let the lamp affix its beam" (CP 64). But now Stevens celebrates not life's completion but life's process. His vision has brought him into contact with "the very thing"—the generative center of the universe, the rock of reality stripped of the deadness of metaphysical imagery and stale category. This is Stevens' moment of aesthetic rapture, akin to the rapture of the beatific vision and the visions of the saints, when his imagination recognizes that its energy issues from a nucleus both holy and powerful, from the very source of reality's energy:

> Look at it in its essential barrenness
> And say this, this is the centre that I seek.
> Fix it in an eternal foliage
>
> And fill the foliage with arrested peace,
> Joy of such permanence, right ignorance
> Of change still possible.

(CP 373)

Here is Stevens in his most assertive moment, detailing as specifically as he can how he finds cause in a barren universe for hope and freedom. They issue from the barrenness itself, which equals pure generative energy without the clutter of names. They issue from the realization of the imagination's power not only to locate the center by exiling "desire / For what is not" (CP 373), but then to "fix" it in foliage of the imagination's own creation. The freedom is tantamount to Adam's in Eden but more difficult since Adam was *at* the center while the modern poet must *locate* it by decreation—"Without evasion by a single metaphor"—before re-creation can occur. Stevens uses oxymoronic imagery to establish that the "permanence" of his joy does not intrude upon reality's flux—the "change still possible." For once, fixity is good because the foliage in which the imagination "fixes" the center issues from process itself and therefore always participates in change.

Canto iii confronts the ineffability of the mystical moment and tries, within the limits of language, to supply metaphors that capture the moment's import. In each of the canto's three stanzas, Stevens evolves a structural image as an expression of the vivid center: it is a "natural tower of all the world"; it is "the mountain on which the tower stands, / . . . the final mountain"; finally, it is "the old man standing on the tower, / Who reads no book" (CP 373–74). The natural tower becomes a "point of survey" and an "Axis of everything," from which the old man views in the fulfillment of summer ("green's green apogee") the "refuge that the end creates." Once again, death mothers the world's beauty. Facing his "end," the old man represents a composite of the wisdom of Emerson's fully matured scholar and Thoreau's natural adventurer who, in the lushness of midsummer, ignores his book in order to assimilate nature's primitive wealth: "his ruddy ancientness / Absorbs the ruddy summer and is appeased" (CP 374). An apogee of humanity, he stands upon a mountain in witness to the apogee of the seasons. J. Dennis Huston summarizes the sacred connotations critics have discovered in the image of the mountain:

The mountain, as both Northrop Frye and Mircea Eliade have argued in different contexts, is characteristically a place of epiphany, for its position is between the mutable world of earth and the eternal world of the heavens. And here the mountain has just such symbolic significance. As an *axis mundi*, a connection between heaven and earth located at the center of the world, it translates into space the psychological center mentioned in the second section.[18]

Stevens' mountain, however, serves not as a "connection" to heaven, but as a symbolic platform from which to better perceive earth. "More precious than the view beyond" (CP 373), the tower becomes an altar from which man pays homage to earth after exiling his desire for heaven.

Vendler contends that following the first three cantos, "the oneness with the here and now diminishes, until by the end of the poem Stevens is at an inhuman distance from his starting point."[19] Stevens does, in fact, deviate in cantos iv through vii from the vividness of the present moment described in the initial sections. Since his vision cannot be captured by words, he searches familiar parables through which to convey its impression without destroying its impact. Inevitably, this involves a tangential approach to his subject. In the closing cantos, however, he returns to the visionary moment with a directness that is neither "inhuman" nor distant.

The residue of the vision penetrates canto iv. Stevens travels imaginatively to the Pennsylvania farmland of his youth, a "land too ripe for enigmas" (CP 374), and realizes an important fact:

just as, within reality's cycle, summer's apogee provides sufficient fruit to sustain man throughout the year, so will his redemptive midsummer vision provide parallel sustenance for the imagination's activity:

> Things stop in that direction and since they stop
> The direction stops and we accept what is
> As good. The utmost must be good and is
> And is our fortune and honey hived in the trees
> And mingling of colors at a festival.

(CP 374)

The vision itself has stopped. But its richness and colors can be stored like honey hived in trees to provide winter sweetness. Canto v continues this emphasis on the lasting quality of the perceptive moment. Stevens adapts imagery from the Christian myth to illustrate his thesis: "One day enriches a year. One woman makes / The rest look down. One man becomes a race" (CP 374). As the Christ-God and the virgin-mother combine on Christmas day (the "one day" might be Christmas, Easter, or both) to provide enough spiritual nourishment to sustain Christians throughout the year, the poet's visionary moment will do the same for him. Since there are no images by which to express the center, Stevens uses those details of the Christian myth that parallel his private revelation. Christianity involves revelatory moments, too, and he employs these in the middle cantos of "Credences" not only to assist in the expression of the inexpressible but also to signify the sacred qualities of his experience.

Canto vi takes the image of the "rock" upon which Christ built his church and against which the gates of hell could not prevail and transposes it into a figure for the holy center within a secular paradise:

> The rock cannot be broken. It is the truth.
> It rises from land and sea and covers them.
> It is a mountain half way green. . . .
>
>   .   .   .   .
> It is the visible rock, the audible,
> The brilliant mercy of a sure repose,

> On this present ground, the vividest repose,
> Things certain sustaining us in certainty.
>
> (CP 375)

Like the living church, Stevens' rock is a pulsing, not a static form. Not a "symbol in hermitage" but a visible, vibrant force, the rock is a powerful figure for the "essential barrenness" at the center from which the imagination receives its energy. God-like but not god, it connotes a secular cathedral from which issue "mercy," "repose," and "certainty." It inhabits earth's sea and sky, substituting its awesome particularity for the phantoms of old doctrines.

Canto viii announces a sudden shift of direction: "The trumpet of morning blows in the clouds and through / The sky" (CP 376). The cock's trumpeting heralds the end of summer and ushers in autumnal clouds. Stevens dismisses his parables as "stratagems / Of the spirit" and turns his attention again to the present moment where "what is possible / Replaces what is not" (CP 376). His visionary interlude almost over, he realizes that nature's patterns must follow their inevitable course. The perfect moment cannot be sustained. In the next section, the cock sits on a bean pole, which Huston sees as "another symbol of the *axis mundi*."[20] As barnyard timepiece, the cock represents transience, and what it perceives signals the death of summer:

> With one eye watch the willow, motionless.
> The gardener's cat is dead, the gardener gone
> And last year's garden grows salacious weeds.
>
> A complex of emotions falls apart,
> In an abandoned spot.
>
> (CP 377)

Summer's zenith passes as do the emotional splendors of a visionary moment. Stevens permits his Eden to die because he knows that the revolving patterns will generate other gardens and gardeners, and the cock will worry about another cat. Summer's apogee knows no other course.

But now the imagination operates within its own time scheme, and the death of literal summer no longer implies an end to the imagination's activities. The mind's processes can operate independently of the world's. In the final canto, Stevens establishes a new vision emanating from the discoveries of the original. He creates a fictive garden free of dead cats and salacious weeds, an imaginative Eden inhabited by young, healthy beings expressive of another summer apogee:

> In which the characters speak because they want
> To speak, the fat, the roseate characters,
> Free, for a moment, from malice and sudden cry,
> Complete in a completed scene, speaking
> Their parts as in a youthful happiness.

(CP 378)

The garden's "completed scene" occurs within the mind of the poet who fully realizes that the imagination redeems him from the violence of external reality. This was the message of his midsummer vision. Since he witnesses the world in metaphor, he can create fictive moments within fictive time—moments free from reality's "malice and sudden cry." He finds repose from the world's *mal* in the life of the mind.

In the poems of *The Auroras of Autumn*, Stevens creates out of the "vividest repose" of his visionary discovery in "Credences." He realizes what William James so strenuously emphasized, that "the existence of mystical states absolutely overthrows the pretension of non-mystical states to be the sole and ultimate dictators of what we may believe" (VRE 418). "The Auroras of Autumn" and "An Ordinary Evening in New Haven" project a poet moving comfortably within the processes of his private mental acts. As Riddel observes, Stevens has discovered that "the mind is where reality happens, where one comes finally to live."[21] Moving into his last years, Stevens' affirmation of existence in a world without structure does not falter.

4 IN WINTER'S NICK

The Auroras of Autumn

erle Brown has commented that "American poets have not, in general, aged well, because they have been unwilling to live their agedness with any fullness of being."[1] Wallace Stevens changes that circumstance. His poems in the last two books are of his late sixties and early seventies. Especially in such longer pieces as "The Auroras of Autumn" and "An Ordinary Evening in New Haven," Stevens makes his most energetic attempts to interpenetrate the processes of mind and world. In "Credences," he experienced a vision of the imageless center of his universe and brought forward the discoveries of James and Emerson that the knowing self may attain fleeting glimpses of wholeness in a world of parts and flux. In the poems following upon his vision he was obligated to develop a rhetorical method that could wring approximations from the invisible and central source without sculpturally fixing it. To achieve this, Stevens had to transform the flux of reality into a flowing poetic form, and that is precisely what he accomplishes in "An Ordinary Evening in New Haven." No longer content with linear poems that state a thesis and come to a conclusion, Stevens evolves a new form for poetry as resilient and alive as the world it describes. As an aging man, he expends an enormous imaginative energy in order to enact in a "Pure rhetoric of a language without words" (CP 374) the brilliance of his response to the holy center of existence.

In this central brilliance, Stevens far surpasses the performance of Emerson's generative imagination. As Emerson advanced in age, instead of continuing his lifelong development as a thinking man who adjusts daily the mind's flow to the world's constant change, he increasingly repeated the tenets of his younger years. The repetitions degenerate into an imposed orthodoxy that instead of enlarging upon his philosophy stunts it. Stephen Whicher concludes that Emerson's seminal period ended by 1848, after which he merely reaped the harvest of his youthful wisdom. The portrait Whicher sketches of Emerson as a wise old scholar, benignly optimistic and enterprising, specifies a defeat of the romantic imagination:

We no longer find in his later books either the confusion or the dramatic uncertainty that accompanied the serious adjustments of his earlier thought. The transcendental issue, the crucial question of his early inner life, had been decided; his optimism, immune to experience, had no power of further growth; and now, secure in the arms of the Wise God, nothing remained but to fulfill his vocation and while away his time on earth by drawing the portrait of such lords of life as he could distinguish and by charting the conditions of mortal life and happiness. . . . he has lost only, if it be a loss, a certain sense of unpredictable possibilities, a feeling of immeasurable hope, which gave his earlier writings, in contrast to his later, an air of high romance.[2]

The image of Emerson whiling away his hours contradicts much that a lifetime of imaginative action had established. The defeat of Emerson's imagination in his old age proceeded inevitably from the paradox of a dual commitment to process and to Christianity. Writing from a foundation of orthodoxy, Emerson formulated a philosophy celebrating the independence of the self and of imaginative activity. In the earliest expression of that philosophy, the emancipated self possessed messianic powers, which, properly exercised, could alter the structure of the world by eradicating conformity, consistency, and other forms of sterility and replacing them with the fresh discoveries of an active mind living always in the present moment. But the ruthlessness of the aging process revealed to Emerson that the organic self he espoused could not escape the life-death cycles. "We live, late in life, by memory," he once wrote, "and in our solstices, or periods of stagnation, we live on our memories; as the starved camel lives on his humps" (EJ XIV 325). Trapped within the pervasive religious tenets of his era, the scholar's self-redeeming powers were considerably more limited than he thought. In 1859, Emerson wrote:

It may be that we have no right here as individuals; that the existence of an embodied man marks fall & sin. To be pure, we must live in God radiant & flowing, constituting the health & conservation of the universe. We have stopped, we have stagnated, we have appropriated or become selfish, before we could arrest our immortality into this callus or wen of an individual, and have been punished by the wars, infirmities & fate, of human life. (EJ XIV 337)

Although he rebelled against the fixity of Christian dogma, Emerson did not deny either the notion of God or the redemptive Christ. Therefore, he could not abandon, as Stevens had, the final vestiges of dependence upon orthodox systems to begin the process of redeeming himself within the empirical world. To enjoy the redemption Christianity provided, the Emersonian self could not disclaim Adam's fall into time. While Stevens' redemption took place within the context of his imaginative visions disengaged from reality's time scheme, Emerson had to submit to a transempirical deliverance basically alien to his philosophy. Transcendence defeated, skepticism breeds. As Whicher writes, Emerson learned "of the contrast between the transcendental Self and the actual insignificant individual adrift on the stream of time and circumstance. The Saturnalia of faith was offset by skepticism."[3]

Little wonder then that while the later essays and journals propound the syllables of self-reliance in an ever-changing universe, they fail to determine a convinced position. The aging Emerson commits himself not to his own present and future but to the fruits of a youthful past. His old age then becomes a time of resignation to the necessarily partial nature of processive living. Gradually, Emerson releases his hold on the central position in the universe he had struggled to maintain. At sixty-one, he wrote to Carlyle that "to live too long is the capital misfortune. . . . in these our autumnal days we must await with what firmness we can."[4] As early as 1845, when his skeptical inclination was becoming more and more apparent, he wrote in "Experience" that "nothing is left us now but death. We look to that with a grim satisfaction, saying, There at least is reality that will not dodge us" (CWE III 49). Finally, in 1867, Emerson wrote "Terminus," his poem of acquiescence to aging and fate, in which he admits "It is time to be old, / To take in sail." Trimming sail to "the storm of time," he resolves to "leave the many and hold the few" (CWE IX 251–52). Instead of continuing as an old man the daily adjustment of imagination to process, Emerson capitulates, reigns his enthusiasm, and proceeds on the thrust youthful visions had provided. He reverts to an orthodox philosophy of reverie instead of action.

By refusing to capitulate his artistry to the inevitable physical erosion that accompanies aging and by transforming flux and process into poetic form, Wallace Stevens epitomizes the tradition Emerson had fostered and realizes the greatest achievement of the romantic imagination in modern times. Unlike Emerson, Stevens as an aging man commits himself wholeheartedly to a poetry of process. If the flux of reality is unceasing, then Stevens realized he must devise a form that could manifest simultaneously the flow of the world and the flow of the mind. He knew that the poet's images merely approximate the center that he discovered in a momentary vision in "Credences of Summer." But with each approximation, the poet enacts a ritual of self-creation that insures his attunement to the forward propulsion of reality and to the holy center that generates the thrust of world and mind alike. The imagination contends with the power outside of it by an internal power equal in force. As nature recreates itself out of its own destruction, the imagination reforms itself through the minute-to-minute activity of destroying old images and constructing fresh fictions. Discovering a poetic form to mirror reality's flow, Stevens insures that the life of the mind will not petrify, as happened in Emerson's case, but will progress in phase with the reality on which it sustains itself. J. Hillis Miller captures the elusive essence of which Stevens' new form consists: "He comes to write a poetry of fleeting movement, a poetry in which each phrase has beginning and ending at once. Instead of being a solid piece of machinery interacting with the other parts, every image is a recapitulation of the coming into being of the moment and its disappearance."[5] Stevens' late poetry affirms that there is one continual poem, and that the imagination must never cease from creating it. This was the theory of poetry as a theory of life for which he had been searching all through the period leading up to the fragile political formulas of "Notes."

The new poetic format that Stevens adopted also brings to full expression the pragmatic philosophy of William James. In *Modes of Thought*, Alfred North Whitehead supplies an insight that indicates how James's philosophy applies to the last stage of Stevens' career. Citing James as one of the four great thinkers in Western literature, Whitehead locates the essence of this greatness in a "marvellous sensitivity to the ideas of the present."[6] The sensitivity to the now evolves because James endorses as the primary stage of philosophy not "systematization" but "assemblage." Whitehead expands: "In all systematic thought, there is a tinge of pedantry. There is a putting aside of notions, of experiences, and of suggestions, with the prim excuse that of course we are not thinking of such things. . . . Philosophy can exclude nothing. Thus it should never start from systematization. Its primary stage can be termed *assemblage*."[7] The process of assemblage is unending. It avoids any kind of specialization and attends only to the variety of ideas that arise not from systems of belief but from living in a factual world. Whitehead concludes that James, like all philosophers, could not avoid some systematization: "but above all he assembled. His intellectual life was one protest against the dismissal of experience in the interest of system. He had discovered intuitively the great truth with which modern logic is now wrestling."[8] In short, James had discovered a procedureless philosophy that eliminates terminal conclusions and embraces process. Pragmatism is a philosophy of open form; it assembles the details of reality's flow and constantly reassesses truth in the context of the unceasing accumulation of empirical detail.

Stevens finds the aesthetic counterpart to James's procedureless method in the open form he develops in his late poems. To an increasing degree process becomes not simply an aspect but the subject of Stevens' poetry. As this happens, he rivets the attention of his imagination with more intensity than ever to the world of fact. In "Effects of Analogy," an essay he wrote in the same year as "The Auroras of Autumn," he indicates that a poet's failure to attend to an empirical universe reduces poetry to artificial gesturing: "What is the poet's subject? It is his sense of the world. For him, it is inevitable and inexhaustible. If he departs from it he becomes artificial and laborious and while his artifice may be skillful and his labor perceptive no one knows better than he that what he is doing, under such circumstances, is not essential to him" (NA 121). The true poet can never be distracted from inexhaustible process. Stevens brings forward James's recurring premise that the pragmatist must turn away from verbal solutions and closed systems and turn toward "concreteness and adequacy, towards facts, towards action and towards power" (PR 379). Stevens specifically details the lineaments of poetic power stemming from a pragmatic world:

One relates to the imagination as a power within him not so much to destroy reality at will as to put it to his own uses. He comes to feel that his imagination is not wholly his own but that it may be part of a much larger, much more potent imagination, which it is his affair to try to get at. For this reason, he pushes on and lives, or tries to live . . . on the verge of consciousness. (NA 115)

This restates James's premise that "we live . . . upon the front edge of an advancing wave-crest, and our sense of a determinate direction in falling forward is all we cover of the future of our path" (ERE 206). For Stevens, the verge of consciousness is equivalent to occupying a position always at the crest of the quotidian and adapting a poetic form proportionate to that position. Achieving this, the imagination becomes "a power within him to have such insights into reality as will make it possible for him to be sufficient as a poet in the very center of consciousness. This results . . . in a central poetry" (NA 115). The poetry that includes "The Auroras of Autumn" and "An Ordinary Evening in New Haven" is Stevens' most central poetry, reflecting a tremendous effort to reduce the separation between imagination and reality and "plainly to propound" (CP 389) the particulars of his physical world.

Several critics seriously misjudge Stevens' change in style and find his creative energies running down in his last books. Joseph Riddel considers the late poems overcommitted to inwardness and designates The Auroras of Autumn "a questionable poetry even by generous estimate."[9] Since it is motivated by exhaustion and despair that it does not overcome, Helen Hennessy Vendler thinks "An Ordinary Evening" "the saddest of all Stevens' poems."[10] Vendler praises "The Auroras of Autumn" as a "dazzling performance" as long as it studies the sky and motion but contends that "indoors, it weakens, and it falters in its regressive motion toward childhood, before the serpent entered Eden."[11] Failure to read these poems as the culmination of the traditions of the central man, the processive universe, the empirical world—in other words of the tradition of Emerson and James—prompts critics to overlook the profound affirmation that underlies their difficult progression and to find instead the expected falling off that typifies the writing of most septuagenarians. But the poems defy hasty judgment. They indicate that Stevens is far from senility or from the depression of the erosion of "an old man living in the lack and the blank."[12] In his final years Stevens possesses sufficient clairvoyance to create works of the first order—his most difficult poems to apprehend and the most rewarding to discover.

Discussion of "The Auroras of Autumn" requires some reconsideration of the visionary experience Stevens had in "Credences of Summer." The final cantos of "Credences" express Stevens' realization that the rock of summer must soon fade into autumnal shadings. The imagination cannot linger at the apogee of midsummer without losing the landscape of the real that constantly replenishes its power. The principle of change that transported the mind to summer insures a similar transport to autumn. Clearly, Stevens intends the titles of his last three books, which include references to summer, autumn, and rock, as double indicators of cyclical recurrence on the one hand and of a vibrant imagination advancing toward stillness on the other. Yet the vision in "Credences" has provided Stevens a major variation on the notion of stillness that it will be helpful to review. Natural cycles lead to death-stillness. Therefore if it responds to natural cycles, once winter comes, the imagination must await natural rebirth in spring in order to be able to generate new fictions. But a stillness exists separate from either natural or imaginative cycles. This is the imageless rock, the stillness that "cannot be broken" (CP 375), a savage source from which emanate the powers of mind and world alike. This stillness pertains not to fixity but to sacred *presence*, which William James defines as "*a perception* of what we may call 'something there,' more deep and more general than any of the special and particular 'senses' by which the current psychology supposes existent realities to be originally revealed" (VRE 58). In a vision, Stevens experienced direct contact with a "something there"—an "essential barrenness" at the center of the universe. He called it "rock." His experience repeats Shelley's vision in "Hymn to Intellectual Beauty," when the "awful shadow of some unseen Power" fell suddenly upon him and he dedicated his poetic powers henceforth toward recapturing in words the energy of the holy event. Like Shelley, after "Credences" Stevens directs his poetic energies toward the irradiation of the venerable stillness. Poetry becomes the physical manifestation of the brilliance of invisible presence. By imaginative power acting in unison with the physical universe, Stevens enacts a ritual of transcendence. Since the "unseen Power" not only generates change but reveals itself within change, the imagination always must act within its intimate attachment to the flux of literal reality. Logically, then, Stevens' transport away from summer's ripeness into autumn's decay cannot be construed in any negative sense; it provides but another opportunity for the imagination to evoke a fresh fictive version of reality through which to approach the holiness of the rock. Stevens has learned that "One poem proves another and the whole, / For the clairvoyant men that need no proof" (CP 441). He realizes what James had emphasized, that "the world is full of partial purposes, of partial stories" (SPP 265).

In this context, "The Auroras of Autumn" *proves* the discoveries of "Credences" and together they formulate apt testament to the whole scope of Stevens' poetry. The two poems relate to each other more by difference than by similarity. Whereas "Credences" is a poem of ripeness and daylight, "Auroras" announces decay and night-darkness. Insofar as "Credences" specifies the solidity of summer's balance and the clarity of Stevens' vision, it exhibits an architecture of strong, immobile images—tower, rock, throne, mountain, pole. In "The Auroras," a poem of tentativeness and imbalance, the structures are falling; its imagery is decreative and relentlessly flickering. Pole, hills, nest, and fields float in air; a deserted cabin rots on a dried white beach; a dispossessed father searches for crown and throne that once defined his security. The imagination's eye, which perceived summer's apogee with such rarefied vividness, struggles in autumn to discern stable forms in the sky's spectral yet glorious motion. Stevens opposes "the hottest fire of sight" (CP 373) in his sun-poem to the "frigid brilliances," "blue-red sweeps," and "polar green" (CP 413) of the auroral night. In the aurora borealis he finds the perfect figure to express the natural and psychic shifts that are the subject of his poem. He describes an apogee of autumn equal in power to the one of summer and no less evocative with all its movement of the sacred stillness he had perceived.

As "Credences" opened with a double emphasis on "now," so Stevens begins "The Auroras" with a strong declarative "This is," then repeats the phrase five times within the first stanza:

> This is where the serpent lives, the bodiless.
> His head is air. Beneath his tip at night
> Eyes open and fix on us in every sky.
> . . . .
> This is where the serpent lives. This is his nest,
> These fields, these hills, these tinted distances,
> And the pines above and along and beside the sea.
>
> This is form gulping after formlessness,
> Skin flashing to wished-for disappearances
> And the serpent body flashing without the skin.
>
> (CP 411)

Stevens' "nows" had magnified the relevance of a visionary moment; his echoing "this is" represents the dual effort of the imagination first to attend to the facticity or thisness of its new season
and then to manage some form of linguistic stability in the spinning cosmos. "This" connotes a specificity the imagination does
not yet on this night possess, and its repetition is the poet's first
step toward converting an elusive perception into a satisfying fiction. The Edenic portrait of roseate characters "Complete in a
completed scene" (CP 378) with which "Credences" closed evap-
orates. Now the serpent reenters the garden and the imagination
must assess its import. Stevens establishes quickly that this is not
the snake of Genesis or Milton. It issues from the borealis display
and expresses not evil but good, or at least the evil-good implied
in man's accepting the blessed fate Stevens discovered in "Esthétique du Mal": living fully in a physical world.

> This is the height emerging and its base
> These lights may finally attain a pole
> In the midmost midnight and find the serpent there,
>
> In another nest, the master of the maze
> Of body and air and forms and images,
> Relentlessly in possession of happiness.

                                                    (CP 411)

Form gulping after formlessness describes the relentlessness of
process, and the snake nesting in the pivot of the northern sky
becomes an analogue for the imagination's life as it sloughs old
structures and fashions new ones in perpetual metamorphosis.

As symbol of mutability, the serpent in the sky becomes the poem's controlling image. Stevens' finesse at striking a precise figure
to express his meaning is evident here. The snake slithering through
a modulating sky and the imaginative eye stalking it as though it
were the night's only stable form when in fact it represents flux,
compounds the multifariousness of the image and increases the
rich complexity of the entire poem. The imagination must repeat
the serpent's activity, which indeed it does through the remaining

cantos by confronting the terror of process, subduing it, and finally returning man by means of another imaginative vision to the same state of innocence achieved in the final canto of "Credences of Summer." "The Auroras" revamps the imagination's summer theater, dismisses antiquated props, and invigorates empirical foundations. As Donald Davie observes, since aurora suggests dawn and beginning while autumn connotes eve and ending, the title establishes cyclical pattern as the theme of the work: "In my end is my beginning."[13] The poem's ten meditations represent consecutive sloughings of the imagination's old forms as Stevens makes process not only the subject but the form of the piece. This is Stevens' way of avoiding Emerson's tendency in the final years toward repeating earlier discoveries. By the challenge of seasonal change to supply new images of reality, Stevens redeems the imagination from autumnal stagnation and, in the tradition of radical empiricism, continues to discover salvation in accumulated acts of thought.

The next four cantos create fictive accounts of the rigors of an imagination working to slough the forms of the summer world. Cantos ii, iii and iv open with the phrase "Farewell to an idea" as the mind looks backward and enacts a demythologizing ritual. Stevens already has provided the proper context for understanding these echoing "farewells" in the early poem "Farewell to Florida," in which the imagination announces "the past is dead . . . I am free" (CP 117) and voyages northward with the moon at the masthead. The difference in "Auroras" is that, instead of announcing freedom as an accomplished fact, Stevens elaborates the processes by which freedom is attained. In another early "farewell" poem, "Waving Adieu, Adieu, Adieu," Stevens indicates the strategy of these processes:

> In a world without heaven to follow, the stops
> Would be endings, more poignant than partings, profounder,
> And that would be saying farewell, repeating farewell,
> Just to be there and just to behold.

> (CP 127)

In a changing world, the present imagination must always wave adieu to its earlier forms. The specific "idea" to which the mind gestures farewell in "The Auroras" vacillates like the serpent itself. It involves a composite of the ideas of summer propounded in *Transport to Summer*. On a grander scale, it refers to any conceptual structure that offers deceptive comfort to the imagination by lulling it away from facticity. Stevens construes these comforts in the parable of a deserted cabin on a beach, perhaps a northern version of Crispin's retreat in "The Comedian as the Letter C." Whereas Crispin indulges himself in the cabin's comfort and evolves from shaping poems to concocting doctrine, the poet of "The Auroras" faces in the bleached-white flowers and the sand blowing across the floor clear evidence of the dangers of resisting transience. In order to remain in phase with the procession of the seasons, the mind must abandon the consolations old domiciles provide.

But this cannot be achieved without considerable struggle. In canto iii, the imagination first bids farewell, then instinctively lingers amid the cabin's restful familial scene.

> Farewell to an idea . . . The mother's face,
> The purpose of the poem, fills the room.
> They are together, here, and it is warm,
>
> With none of the prescience of oncoming dreams.
>
> (CP 413)

Contrasting with the bitterness of autumnal weather, the warmth of the mother's image intoxicates the imagination. As "the purpose of the poem" she represents both an old man's reflection upon the pure childhood bliss associated with literal motherhood and the fecund earth as mythological mother of all poets and all poems. The mother "gives transparence" to her family, but, as happens to all of the warm interludes of the past, "she has grown old" (CP 413). Like a lost son peering through an imaginative window, Stevens stands outside of this drama with the sure knowledge that the wind of time will "knock like a rifle-butt against the door" (CP 414) and dissolve the primitive scene. With the children, he must "say good-night, good-night" to the mythological mother and discover transparence in fresher mediums of his own creation.

Cantos iv and v provide a much harsher meditation on the mythological father figure. Whereas the mother inhabits earth, the father "assumes the great speeds of space" and "leaps from heaven to heaven more rapidly / Than bad angels leap from heaven to hell in flames" (CP 414). The warm earth-mother and cold sky-father specify the roots of man's alienation both within himself and in his natural environment. Vendler observes that the father is "descended from the outmoded Jehovah figures, giants, mythy Joves, and so on. . . ."[14] As one who authoritatively "says no to no and yes to yes" (CP 414), he is also the offspring of James's "rationalist": "your devotee to abstract and eternal principles . . . of dogmatic temper in his affirmations" (PR 364–65). Dissatisfied by the loss of his mythical significance, the father loses himself in a fictive reverie completely detached from the physical universe. He "fetches tellers of tales," "negresses to dance," and "pageants out of air" (CP 415) in a feeble attempt to realign himself with his world. Stevens' father embodies an imaginative projection of man's need for a rationalist-god whose mythy nature may have been good for a time but who finally becomes completely separated from his feminine counterpart, the empirical earth-mother. The once "Master O master seated by the fire" (CP 414) recedes to an absent father-god who possesses neither home nor heaven and who moves ever farther from the searching children who lost control of their own creation. Stevens emphatically rejects the father's imaginative travesty, referring to it as "loud, disordered mooch" (CP 415). Renouncing this father and his empty myths, Stevens renounces all forms of organized religion and the solace they might provide in his movement through autumn into winter.

Canto vi juxtaposes the father's foolish "festival" with the awesome brilliance of the northern lights:

> It is a theatre floating through the clouds,
> Itself a cloud, although of misted rock
> And mountains running like water, wave on wave,
>
> Through waves of light.
>
> (CP 416)

Now Stevens completely abandons summer's fictions—the cabin and its family—and releases his imagination into the autumn sky. What follows is an exquisite rendering of a mind in the act of formulating linguistic versions of the processive beauty it perceives. Nature's solidity succumbs to the dissolving power of the lights as rock, clouds, mountains, and waves mesh into a single primal element called change. Animating a macabre scene, the poet's words range freely from image to image as the mind, like the auroral cloud, "drifts idly through half-thought-of forms" (CP 416).

Suddenly, in the midst of total immersion in the borealis, the imagination arrests its frolic and formulates a central conclusion of the poem:

> This is nothing until in a single man contained,
> Nothing until this named thing nameless is
> And is destroyed. He opens the door of his house
>
> On flames. The scholar of one candle sees
> An Arctic effulgence flaring on the frame
> Of everything he is. And he feels afraid.
>
> (CP 416–17)

The "scholar of one candle" is Emerson's "Poet." Unless the awesome spectacle of the world's metamorphosis is translated by the single man as poet into linguistic form, it has no significance. Stevens expands upon the very image Emerson had used to illustrate the poet's enervating powers. After listening as a boy to the genius of a new young poet, Emerson exclaimed in "The Poet" that "we sat in the aurora of a sunrise which was to put out all the stars." He continued: "I had fancied that the oracles were all silent, and nature had spent her fires; and behold! all night, from every pore, these fine auroras have been streaming" (CWE III

10-11). For both writers, the auroras signify the energy and beauty comprising process. Stevens expresses again the decreative urgency involved in the poet's world. Man has tamed the magnificence of the spectacle by fixing it within the verbal form "aurora borealis." Only by destroying the named thing and rendering it nameless again can the scholar-poet contain what would otherwise be nothing within a fresh form.

The poet "feels afraid" because the infinite candlepower of nature's energetic flux seems no match for the single candle of his own consciousness, which somehow must translate within endless cycles the "Arctic effulgence flaring on the frame / Of everything he is" (CP 417). The single man opening "the door of his house / On flames" and merging his diminutive energy with the energy of the night restates Stevens' old subject of the interpenetration of the process of mind and world. His imagery strikingly parallels Emerson's in "The Poet":

beside his privacy of power as an individual man, there is a great public power on which he can draw, by unlocking, at all risks, his human doors, and suffering the ethereal tides to roll and circulate through him; then he is caught up into the life of the Universe, his speech is thunder, his thought is law, and his words are universally intelligible. (CWE III 26-27)

Clearly, Emerson describes here another visionary moment that "The Auroras of Autumn" repeats. By unlocking the doors of the house that the imagination of summer built and destroying all its images, Stevens becomes "caught up into the life" of autumn. He discovers in the auroras an *axis mundi* parallel to summer's apogee. Diminished to an inconsiderable speck within nature's terrible energy, the imagination confronts the spectacle with what force it can muster by creating new structures by which to name the nameless season. In this fashion, the mind redeems itself from the fall away from the Edenic garden of "roseate characters" in "Credences" that the coming of autumn had caused and regains the fresh stage of innocence that is the subject of cantos viii-x. The poet, writes Emerson, "uses forms according to the life, and not according to the form" (CWE III 21). Stevens infuses the

imagination with new vitality by attending to nature's forms and
interpolating them through words.

Canto viii indicates the extent to which the flickering form of
the northern lights has been transposed into the form of the
poem. In the approximations of rhetoric, statements shift and
flash as one minute's assertion proceeds into the next minute's
qualification or retraction. The serpentine movement of Stevens'
subordinate clauses indicates the borealis nests in the mind as well
as in the sky. Despite its shimmering qualities, this stanza asserts
the presence of a state of pure innocence that the exhibition of
lights helps to define:

> So, then, these lights are not a spell of light,
> A saying out of a cloud, but innocence.
> An innocence of the earth and no false sign
>
> Or symbol of malice.
>
> (CP 418)

The imagination dispels the magical qualities that pertain to the
spectacle, causing so much fear, and perceives it without false
signs or symbols. The purity of a mind relieved of old distortions
and formulations engenders the innocence by which the imagination can continue to generate redeeming fictions. Stevens implies
that the loss of the "arrested peace" that the imagination had
achieved in summer's garden was the result of the inability to perceive the world directly. By falling out of phase, the imagination
lost its original relationship to the world. When the mind unclut-
ters itself, it rediscovers an

> innocence
> As pure principle.
> . . . like a thing of ether that exists
> Almost as predicate. But it exists,
> It exists, it is visible, it is, it is.
>
> (CP 418)

Having achieved proper realignment with reality, the imagination
reforms the mother and children rejected in canto iii:

> Lie down like children in this holiness,
> As if, awake, we lay in the quiet of sleep,
>
> As if the innocent mother sang in the dark
> Of the room and on an accordion, half-heard,
> Created the time and place in which we breathed.
>   (CP 418–19)

To celebrate its attunement, the imagination creates a fictive scene to replace the one it lost. The mother returns as the creative principle, the purpose for autumn's poem as she was for summer's. Again she "fills the room," which now is no cabin, but the dark room of night under the transparence of a splendid sky.

Canto ix extends the imagination's vision of innocence. As in "Esthétique du Mal" and "Credences," Stevens describes a paradise regained "in the idiom of an innocent earth, / Not of the enigma of the guilty dream" (CP 419). To the paradisaical scene, he brings an integrated community of hale-hearted landsmen, a self-composed and self-sufficient family reminiscent of the "ring of men" that chanted in orgy in "Sunday Morning:"

> We thought alike
> And that made brothers of us in a home
> In which we fed on being brothers, fed
>
> And fattened as on a decorous honeycomb.
>   (CP 419)

The mother as feminine principle of the imagination insures the cohesion of the communal scene when she unites with a male principle that replaces the mythy father of canto iv:

> The rendezvous, when she came alone,
> By her coming became a freedom of the two,
> An isolation which only the two could share.
>   (CP 419)

The mother commingles with the masculine night, belted and clothed in flashing stars, and the seminal balance of imagination with reality is achieved. Stevens culminates a vision of another Eden of characters who "speak because they want / To speak" since they are "Complete in a completed scene" (CP 378). But he does not close his midnight meditation on the moment of ful-fillment as he had done in his credence-poem of high noon. If the imagination fell out of Eden once, it will happen again and again. In the midst of fictive bliss, Stevens anticipates the mind's next disaster in vivid terms: "Shall we be found hanging in the trees next spring? / Of what disaster is this the imminence" (CP 419). The flashing skies have taught the mind anticipation but not re-gret. The mind assimilates the process that imagination and real-ity, the Eve and Adam of this new garden, must be divorced again as a natural aspect of cyclical process. In spring, the commu-nal honeycomb might hang amid "Bare limbs, bare trees and a wind as sharp as salt" (CP 419) but the likelihood of that calam-ity is not cause for depression. Disaster mothers innocence as well as beauty:

> It may come tomorrow in the simplest word,
> Almost as part of innocence, almost,
> Almost as the tenderest and the truest part.
>
> (CP 420)

In the height of vision, Stevens perceives the wholeness involved in process. He finds something terrifying in the realization that disaster comes nonchalantly, "in the simplest word," but as long as the imagination can redeem itself from calamity to create fresh honeycombs in the landscape of its own fictions, then calamity becomes but one of the particulars in the glittering flux.

Innocence once sealed in change, canto x considers the process of meditation itself. As Harold Bloom suggests, this sequence "is a poetic apologia that concludes by returning us to the wind and to the flaring auroras that we now see have never been absent from the poem."[15] The mind retreats from the center of the flaring "Arctic effulgence" (CP 417) to consider a perspective for its experience and then to "solemnize the secretive syllables" (CP 420) of its conclusion. Stevens rejects as the milieu of his poetic domain either a too dreary ("An unhappy people in an unhappy world" [CP 420]) or a too cheerful ("A happy people in a happy world" [CP 420]) extreme. The mind settles on a condition consistent to the details of its vision—"An unhappy people in a happy world"—in which peace and disaster operate in tandem. Davie misrepresents this option as Stevens' decision "that man's destiny is as it is because God requires in His Creation, before it can satisfy Him, an element of conflict to be reconciled, and hence a margin of freedom for man that leaves him capable of heroism."[16] God is no part of this picture except in Stevens' sense that "God and the imagination are one" (CP 524), which is not how Davie interprets it. The god of this canto and indeed of the entire poem is the "scholar of one candle" or Emersonian poet. Through this fiction ("This contrivance of the spectre of the spheres" [CP 420]) he has fulfilled his meditations in "Contriving balance to contrive a whole" (CP 420). The scholar-poet subdues his fear of the awesome creativity in the natural world by enacting parallel creative acts that reconcile world change and mind change. The "contrivance" of the achieved balance is not reason for despair but signifies an aspect of the willingness to rest final belief in a fiction. "The Auroras," then, strongly supports Stevens' contention that each poetic act "is an illumination of a surface, the movement of a self in the rock" (OP 241). As was the case with the mountain of summer, he discerns in autumn's rock vibrations sufficient to sustain him:

> As if he lived all lives, that he might know,
>
> In hall harridan, not hushful paradise,
> To a haggling of wind and weather, by these lights
> Like a blaze of summer straw, in winter's nick.
>
> (CP 420–21)

Joyfully, the poet accepts as the replacement of the "hushful paradise" of old myths the "hall harridan" of autumn. By the single candle of poetic consciousness standing on the threshold of winter's disaster, the mind "meditates a whole" (CP 420) in the pluralism. The regeneration of Emerson's poet is complete:

the poet turns the world to glass, and shows us all things in their right series and procession. For through that better perception he stands one step nearer to things, and sees the flowing or metamorphosis; perceives that thought is multiform; that within the form of every creature is a force impelling it to ascend into a higher form; and following with his eyes the life, uses the forms which express that life, and so his speech flows with the flowing of nature. (CWE III 20–21)

Emerson's description highlights the essence of Stevens' technique in "The Auroras of Autumn." The forms of nature interpenetrate the forms of the mind; trying to find what will suffice, the poet then embodies his fiction in the form of words. The "never-failing genius" (CP 420) at the core of the procedure is change. In an address delivered a few years after the publication of "Auroras," Stevens identified the genius of poetry as "the spirit of visible and invisible change" (OP 242). This late in his life, he realized that no matter what its effects on the body, process vitalizes the mind whether the mind is in winter's nick or summer's apogee. Defining the "apt locale of the genius of poetry" (CP 242), Stevens provides a fit summation to a discussion of "The Auroras": "Its position is always an inner position, never certain, never fixed. It is to be found beneath the poet's word and deep within the reader's eye in those chambers in which the genius of poetry sits alone with her candle in a moving solitude" (OP 243).

After an extraordinary evening of realism in "The Auroras," Stevens turns in his last long poem to the commonplaces of "An Ordinary Evening in New Haven." The season remains autumn but the cabin and honeycomb and flashing effulgence are replaced by a somewhat drab rainy evening under a blank sky without even a moon. In a letter to Bernard Heringman, Stevens sets a proper context for a reading of the poem:

At the moment I am at work on a thing called An Ordinary Evening In New Haven. This is confidential and I don't want the thing to be spoken of. But here my interest is to try to get as close to the ordinary, the commonplace and the ugly as it is possible for a poet to get. It is not a question of grim reality but of plain reality. The object is of course to purge oneself of anything false. . . . This is not in any sense a turning away from the ideas of Credences of Summer: it is a development of those ideas. That sort of thing might ultimately lead to another phase of what you call a seasonal sequence but certainly it would have nothing to do with the weather: it would have to do with the drift of one's ideas. (LWS 636–37)

Stevens published the original version of "An Ordinary Evening" in eleven cantos. By the time the definitive poem was published, the initial form had blossomed into thirty-one cantos, the additional twenty cantos expanding or supporting the themes of the original eleven-canto poem.

Following Stevens' advice, to read "An Ordinary Evening" as a continuation of the ideas of "Credences" requires an explicit affirmation of the "essential barrenness" at the center of reality and of the power of the imagination to fix it in foliage. But the peculiar nature of Stevens' celebration and the apparent formlessness of his final form have caused critics to miss the poem's true mark and to find it a piece of "grim reality" anyway, emanating from the somber mind of a man close to death. Merle Brown, whose comments on the work are otherwise perceptive, displays considerable dearth of empathy in suggesting that while "The Auroras of Autumn" is for him the great poem of Stevens' last period, "An Ordinary Evening" "might well appear to be even greater to an elderly reader."[17] Does Brown mean to imply that the younger reader of Stevens preserves a more accurate slant on the poems? Or that he himself might be too young to estimate the greatness of Stevens' poem of old age? In either case, his is not the only reading of "An Ordinary Evening in New Haven" that overstresses Stevens' physical condition as an ingredient essential to the poem's mood. He goes so far as to suggest that in the thirty-first and final canto, the poetic voice falters to such a degree that "perhaps the poet has dozed off."[18] Helen Hennessy Vendler states the point more severely. To her, "An Ordinary Evening" represents "the harshest of all . . . experiments" of a man who "himself a skeleton, examines the bare possibilities of a skeletal life."[19] (A 1953 photograph of a robust Stevens sitting with his grandson reveals that, as late as four years after writing the poem, Stevens could not be designated, even in a figurative sense, "skeletal" [cf.

LWS Plate XVII]). Vendler continues her estimate: "Stevens is cruelly stringent and sets a desolate scene; the poem cannot hope, under these conditions, to overcome entirely the exhaustion and despair that motivate it. . . . *An Ordinary Evening* is, in short, almost unremittingly minimal, and over and over again threatens to die of its own starvation."[20] Harold Bloom reverses Vendler, arguing that the poem "is threatened not by its own starvation but by its own copiousness, its abundance of invention that varies the one theme."[21] Bloom writes the most thorough as well as the most enthusiastic of the few full-length studies of the poem, yet even he discerns elements of poetic decline in it, agreeing with Vendler that it exhibits "much harshness" and "some deprivation." He conveniently disposes of the contradictory valuations of the piece by averring that "critics can diverge absolutely on this poem because the text is almost impossible to read, that is, the text keeps seeking 'reality' while continually putting into question its own apotheosis of 'reality.' "[22]

This discussion will show that when "An Ordinary Evening in New Haven" is read as a culmination of the tradition of Emerson and James, a large segment of the critical bluster about it dissolves. Rather than being the statement of a decrepit and despairing poet, it is Stevens' triumphant expression of process, his most honest poem and the one most attentive to the ordinariness of empirical living.

Clearly stating as his poem's object "to purge oneself of anything false" (LWS 636), Stevens reveals the extent to which truth, not aging, is his prime concern. As Bloom suggests, ordinary means "true." "An Ordinary Evening" evolves a pragmatic meaning of truth. James's theory of the process of truth validates the poem's open form and verifies its achievement. The core statement of James's thesis bears repeating: "The truth of an idea is not a stagnant property inherent in it. Truth *happens* to an idea. It *becomes* true, is *made* true by events. Its verity *is* in fact an event, a process: the process namely of its verifying itself, its veri-*fication*" (PR 430). Truth then is a concept that continually must be verified by percepts, that is by objects perceived in reality's continuous flux. The pragmatist's notion of truth involves "the way in which one moment in our experience may lead us towards other moments which it will be worth while to have been led to. . . . the truth of a state of mind means this function of *a leading that is worth while*" (PR 431–32). James portrays the thoughts and beliefs that comprise truth as living on a tenuous "credit system." We trade each other's truths as long as they are verifiable in facticity; "but this all points to direct face-to-face verifications somewhere, without which the fabric of truth collapses like a financial system with no cash-basis whatever" (PR 433). In other words, Stevens' wish to purge himself of anything false requires the endless return of the mind to the cash-basis of reality. This brings us to the core of "An Ordinary Evening in New Haven":

> We keep coming back and coming back
> To the real: to the hotel instead of the hymns
> That fall upon it out of the wind. We seek
>
> The poem of pure reality, untouched
> By trope or deviation, straight to the word,
> Straight to the transfixing object, to the object
>
> At the exactest point at which it is itself,
> Transfixing by being purely what it is,
> A view of New Haven, say, through the certain eye,
>
> The eye made clear of uncertainty, with the sight
> Of simple seeing, without reflection. We seek
> Nothing beyond reality.
>
> (CP 471)

Stevens enacts an elaborate verification process in which the imagination comes back to reality and its transfixing objects no less than thirty-one times. He begins each poem at the point where mind and reality touch—the point of experience in its most fundamental form—then elaborates brief mental constructs that, because of their tendency to tempt the mind beyond reality, must immediately be discarded as mind and reality touch again. Since reality merely flows and displays no connectives that define be-

ginning, middle, and end, Stevens' poem also flows minus logical
connectives—without "trope or deviation." The mind creates
poems from the immediacy of what it sees. Because what it sees is
always changing, the life of the mind is a "never-ending meditation" (CP 465), an "endlessly elaborating poem" (CP 486). "An
Ordinary Evening" intrudes upon the endless meditation at an
arbitrary point then withdraws from it the same way. As the
mind's meditations proceed unceasingly, in a sense the poem both
precedes and continues after its own articulation. James illustrates
this when he notes that our fields of experience consist "of process
and transition" and "have no more definite boundaries than have
our fields of view. Both are fringed forever by a *more* that continuously develops, and that continuously supersedes them as life
proceeds" (ERE 207). The "truth" of Stevens' poem involves the
process of one fictive moment leading into the fringes of another
and then another. Stevens affirms the mind's freedom to live
wholly within its own perception of reality or, more specifically,
within the imagination's fictive ideas of the physical world. As
part of the cyclical patterns of destruction and creation, in every
"recent imagining of reality" (CP 465) a fresh fictive truth replaces the former—"a second giant kills the first" (CP 465)—and
internal and external balance is maintained. Again, James illustrates the controlling principle:

The essential thing is the process of being guided. Any idea that helps
us to *deal*, whether practically or intellectually, with either the reality
or its belongings, that doesn't entangle our progress in frustrations,
that *fits*, in fact, and adapts our life to the reality's whole setting, will
agree sufficiently to meet the requirement. It will hold true of that
reality. (PR 435)

To implement ideas agreeable to reality, Stevens compels his
imagination to act at the threshold of consciousness or as near as
possible to what James refers to as "the instant field of the present" (ERE 208). "An Ordinary Evening" develops the premise
that "The poem is the cry of its occasion, / Part of the res itself
and not about it" (CP 473). Since the "occasion" never is fixed,

then any fictive idea "fits" reality's truth only within brief flicks of time. The incompletion of the poem attests to the mind's freedom. Through a process of constant shaping, the mind adheres to reality by refusing to pause within the comfort of its own analogies or those of others. In no other poem is the activity of Stevens' imaginative hounding of reality more aggressive or more intense.

In the context of James's theory of truth, "An Ordinary Evening in New Haven" expresses the vibrancy of the mind's incessant adjustment to change. It is Stevens' purest statement of the meaning of pragmatic existence. New Haven represents an ordinary industrial town in a country of common people whose histories evolve through a series of uneventful rainy evenings in autumn. The city becomes Stevens' rendition of Anderson's Winesburg, Faulkner's Yoknapatawpha County, Masters' Spoon River—a commonplace milieu where the imagination contemplates a reality fecund in the particulars of processive living. New Haven is simply a place for the imagination plainly to be. The rain, the dilapidated houses, and the statues have no mythology. They merely *are*. In "The Auroras of Autumn" Stevens positioned a diminutive mind against an awesome cosmos. In "An Ordinary Evening," he inverts the procedure by reducing the cosmos to a minuscule dot on the map of North America where change is no less violent than it was in the spheres and where the energies of the single candle of consciousness are equally essential to the transformation of process into poetic form.

If the controlling philosophy of the poem is Jamesian, its basic premise is Emersonian and originates in the essay "Circles." In "An Ordinary Evening," Stevens consummates his desire to move from the edge to the center—from a position on the circumference of the circle to its still point. "Esthétique du Mal" expresses this desire in the imagery of "in-bar" and "ex-bar" (CP 317) whereas in "Credences of Summer" it appears in the figure of the "thrice concentred self" (CP 376). Now Stevens borrows directly from Emerson to indicate the relationship between physical and psychical circularity. Stevens' opening statement—"The eye's plain version is a thing apart, / The vulgate of experience" (CP 465)— rephrases the famous opening of "Circles": "The eye is the first circle; the horizon which it forms is the second; and throughout nature this primary figure is repeated without end. It is the highest emblem in the cipher of the world" (CWE II 301). A poem of eyes, "An Ordinary Evening" plays upon numerous aspects of the point of vision "set deep in the eye, / Behind all actual seeing, in the actual scene" (CP 467). From the Latin *vulgatus* meaning "common" or "usual," Stevens' "vulgate" mirrors Emerson's horizon, the second circle of the commonplace world that, in corroboration with the physical eye, the eye of imagination constantly forms. Emerson elaborates the perpetuity of the central eye's activity: "Our life is an apprenticeship to the truth that around every circle another can be drawn; that there is no end in nature, but every end is a beginning; that there is always another dawn risen on mid-noon, and under every deep a lower deep opens" (CWE II 301). Again, Stevens rephrases Emerson. Adapting the biblical boundaries for the all-encompassing God, he represents the beginning and the end as "naked Alpha" and "hierophant Omega." Like the Old Testament God, the imagination oversees the full spectrum of experience and insures the reduction of multifaceted mythologies of the end to the purity of initial perception:

> Reality is the beginning not the end,
> Naked Alpha, not the hierophant Omega,
> Of dense investiture, with luminous vassals.
>
> It is the infant A standing on infant legs,
> Not twisted, stooping, polymathic Z,
>
> . . . .
>
> But that's the difference: in the end and the way
> To the end. Alpha continues to begin.
> Omega is refreshed at every end.

> (CP 469)

James offers a possible source for Stevens' imagery here when he states in "Pragmatism and Humanism" that "the toughminded are the men whose alpha and omega are *facts*. Behind the bare phenomenal facts . . . there is *nothing*" (PR 458).

Nearing life's end, Stevens returns to beginnings by completing the geographical circle of the imagination from North to South to North again. New Haven is a northern city of dense investiture and rigid mythology that the imagination decreates to the commonplace in order to achieve the refreshment of naked Alpha, the in-bar vision of the rock. The poem returns to the first circle of original perception—to the reality of "ever early candor" (CP 382) and discovers with Emerson a fluid and volatile universe in which culture's apparent permanence reflects only an absence of creative insight: "Our culture is the predominance of an idea which draws after it this train of cities and institutions. Let us rise into another idea; they will disappear" (CWE II 302).

"The eye's plain version" which Stevens elaborates in the first canto signifies another visionary instant. "A thing apart" from fictions already formed, the eye's immediate perception catches plainness before foliage, chaos at the very point of form. The mind cannot resist transferring the vision into words: "Of this, / A few words, an and yet, and yet, and yet—" (CP 465). By playful rhetorical stuttering, Stevens prefigures the poem's method. Each canto proliferates from the initial insight as the poem proceeds organically from the center of the eye's plain version outward toward more elaborate fictive forms. The imagination adds to, qualifies, and subordinates until its "few words" finally extend to thirty-one stanzas. As Merle Brown notices, most of the cantos begin with a brief declarative statement about some simple thing then fashion it into something more intricate and mysterious.[23]

Ever so carefully, Stevens examines in the remainder of the first canto the relationship of mind to facticity, the dualism that constitutes the eye's plain version. The "house" of the imagination is composed of "These houses, these difficult objects" (CP 465), the real particulars of New Haven. With each "recent imagining of reality," the mind forms a "new resemblance of the sun" or finds a new mythological structure in which to contain perception. It creates:

> A larger poem for a larger audience,
>
> As if the crude collops came together as one,
> A mythological form, a festival sphere,
> A great bosom, beard and being, alive with age.
>
> (CP 465–66)

In a poem of cycles and circles, the "festival sphere" enjoys a rich, multifarious reference. It is first an ocular sphere, the "exquisite eye" (CP 468) as first circle, where activity of imagination (the internal sphere) originates. Next, as "A great bosom" alive with age, it suggests mother earth—the actual globe or arc of the horizon that the eye forms. Finally, it stands for the poet's own fluid form, the poem he creates in which to contain reality's festive scene. The "festival sphere" becomes a clarifying symbol in this ultimate poem of process. Like Emerson, Stevens uses a sphere to portray the life of the imagination as a "self-evolving circle, which, from a ring imperceptibly small, rushes on all sides outwards to new and larger circles, and that without end" (CWE II 304).

Canto ii conjectures further on the source of the "eye's plain version." The houses of New Haven become the parts of a city in the mind:

> Suppose these houses are composed of ourselves,
> So that they become an impalpable town, full of
> Impalpable bells, transparencies of sound,
>
> Sounding in transparent dwellings of the self.
>
> (CP 466)

The poet seeks a relationship between the mind's eye and the reality it perceives but can locate no dividing line between them. Does the mind *know* what is there, or does it *make* what is there? Stevens decides the moment of "visionary love" (CP 466) involves an intimate co-mixture of subject and object, a "Coming together in a sense in which we are poised, / Without regard to time or where we are" (CP 466). The evocation of timelessness—James's prime ingredient for the occurrence of a mystical experi-

ence—assures the vision. The interrelation of "the perpetual reference" (object) and "the perpetual meditation" (subject) produces the central perception of "The plainness of plain things"
(CP 467). At this point of vision, reality is so much a part of the
mind the two are indistinguishable:

> the indefinite,
> Confused illuminations and sonorities,
> So much ourselves, we cannot tell apart
> The idea and the bearer-being of the idea.
>
> (CP 466)

Later, Stevens will find that "Real and unreal are two in one:
New Haven / Before and after one arrives" (CP 485). Joseph
Riddel observes that after the first two cantos, the remaining
twenty-nine are "concerned primarily with the variable and possible relations of the two opposites, the variety of balances possible in the imaginative life which seeks always the ultimate order,
the conjunction of idea and its bearer-being."[24]

When considered in the context of James's empirical philosophy, those parts of "An Ordinary Evening in New Haven" in
which critics discover evidence of Stevens' disillusion become instead statements of acceptance. James writes:

It is then perfectly possible to accept sincerely a drastic kind of a universe from which the element of 'seriousness' is not to be expelled.
Whoso does so is, it seems to me, a genuine pragmatist. He is willing
to live on a scheme of uncertified possibilities which he trusts; willing
to pay with his own person, if need be, for the realization of the ideals
which he frames. (PR 471)

Stevens commits his entire poem to the mind's fictions, uncertified possibilities that define his whole poetry. He portrays the
effort of the mind to perceive the plainness of reality in terms of a
serious, even "drastic" struggle:

> The plainness of plain things is savagery.
>
> . . . .
>
> . . . Plain men in plain towns
>
> . . . .

> . . . only know a savage assuagement cries
> With a savage voice.

(CP 467)

Ordinary men seeking plain reality are always in danger of being
"snuffed out" "in a great grinding / Of growling teeth" (CP
467). But acceptance of the pluralism obviates despair and prevents a compromise to fixity. In the savagery of the struggle with
reality, man finds appeasement:

> in that cry they hear
> Themselves transposed, muted and comforted
> In a savage and subtle and simple harmony.

(CP 467–68)

The pragmatic imagination, which is always "uncomfortable away
from facts" (PR 385) keeps coming back to the "inescapable
romance, inescapable choice" (CP 468) of reality where the ideals
that it frames are founded.

Stevens construes the imagination's incessant struggle to maintain clarity of vision in other than savage terms as well. If reality
is man's antagonist, it can also be his lover:

> We fling ourselves, constantly longing, on this form.
> We descend to the street and inhale a health of air
> To our sepulchral hollows. Love of the real
>
> Is soft in three-four cornered fragrances.

(CP 470)

We assuage the hollows of being by returning the mind to its
natural lover, reality. Yet the imagination's desire for its empirical
mate is never fully satisfied. Sometimes the nature of process "infuriates our love" because there remains "Always an emptiness
that would be filled" (CP 467). Filling the emptiness, however,
implies existential death since the mind's satisfaction means the
mind's inertia. Stevens contrasts the "permanence composed of
impermanence" (CP 472) upon which the living imagination
feeds with the emptiness of the bronzed man in the moon "whose
mind was made up and who, therefore, died" (CP 472). If

change never fulfills, neither does it stratify; while it infuriates, it provides life's gaiety and joy:

> So that morning and evening are like promises kept,
> So that the approaching sun and its arrival,
> Its evening feast and the following festival,
>
> This faithfulness of reality, this mode,
> This tendance and venerable holding-in
> Make gay the hallucinations in surfaces.

(CP 472)

Stevens made clear in his comments about the poem to Bernard Heringman that the seasonal aspect of "An Ordinary Evening in New Haven" had "nothing to do with the weather" but concerned instead "the drift of one's ideas" (LWS 637). His statement overtly acknowledges the discovery in "Credences" that one's ideas could drift in a metaphorical time scheme similar to but not the same as reality's seasonal patterns. Again and again, within a temporal sequence specific to the imagination's life, Stevens' cantos formulate approximations of the rock of autumn:

> . . . The hibernal dark that hung
> In primavera, the shadow of bare rock,
>
> Becomes the rock of autumn, glittering,
> Ponderable source of each imponderable,
> The weight we lift with the finger of a dream.

(CP 476)

The experience of generating poems of the center is a joyful one especially in light of the mind's freedom from autumn's literal decay. Passing from one example of the rock to the next, the imagination redeems itself within the flux. This "endlessly elaborating poem" then becomes endlessly redemptive too as the mind delights in its own ingenuity at generating "in the intricate evasions of as" (CP 486), fictive versions of "The brilliancy at the central of the earth" (CP 473).

All this considered, it remains especially difficult to accept Vendler's response to canto xvi, in which Stevens writes: "And

yet the wind whimpers oldly of old age / In the western night"
(CP 477). "These whimpers," Vendler argues, "are Stevens' own
human voice turned beaten beast, the voice of the inner and ultimate dilapidation, an incoherence as the Rock crumbles to
dust."[25] As generative core of reality and the imagination both,
by its nature the rock cannot crumble. Stevens' own death will
substantiate not destroy it. The significance of death in "An Ordinary Evening" remains what it has always been to Stevens—the
ultimate stillness that mothers the mind's beautiful forms. The
mothering is never more intense than in this long poem, but to
find Stevens reduced by death's imminence to a "beaten beast"
misses the point, perhaps because it mistakes the writer's own
death fears for the poet's. As a figure for time, Stevens' wind does
whimper a reminder that aging brings death, yet this has been a
factor on the fringe of all of Stevens' poems from *Harmonium* to
The Rock. For the subject of death to disappear as Stevens approaches its reality would constitute a serious evasion, of which
he is not guilty. Similarly, its mere presence in the context of old
age does not constitute morbid preoccupation with "ultimate
dilapidation." Stevens faces autumn's change squarely and finds
death in it the same way he finds rain and houses in New Haven:

> In the area between is and was are leaves,
> Leaves burnished in autumnal burnished trees
> And leaves in whirlings in the gutters.

> (CP 474)

Another commonplace of reality's wheel, death simply *is*, and
physical man cannot evade the import of the leaves' burnishings.
    But imaginative man can. The best response to Vendler's mis-
reading may be found in the voice of canto xxx, which illustrates
in one of the most amazing visions of the entire poem how Stevens
frees the mind from winter's web:

> The last leaf that is going to fall has fallen.
> The robins are là-bas, the squirrels, in tree-caves,
> Huddle together in the knowledge of squirrels.

The wind has blown the silence of summer away.
It buzzes beyond the horizon or in the ground:
In mud under ponds, where the sky used to be reflected.

The barrenness that appears is an exposing.
It is not part of what is absent, a halt
For farewells, a sad hanging on for remembrances.

It is a coming on and a coming forth.
The pines that were fans and fragrances emerge,
Staked solidly in a gusty grappling with rocks.

The glass of the air becomes an element—
It was something imagined that has been washed away.
A clearness has returned. It stands restored.

It is not an empty clearness, a bottomless sight.
It is a visibility of thought,
In which hundreds of eyes, in one mind, see at once.

(CP 487–88)

Hardly "beaten," the imagination discovers here an autumnal replica of the "essential barrenness" or rock of "Credences." Subdued yet distinctly positive, Stevens announces that autumn is not what people think or even what he once thought. It is not a final phase, but the proper season for the imagination's continuing life. It connotes exposition and emergence, not decay and destruction. Summer's loss is not mourned, for the mind composes itself in the power of summer's contrary. Released by its own time scheme from winter's stillness, the imagination contemplates the scenery of autumn—the leaflessness, the hibernation, the fresh symmetry of naked forms—and "stands restored." Autumn's facticity provides the same impetus as summer's had provided; the mind is overwhelmed by hundreds of the "eye's plain version" of the new season. The process of generating new fictions to embody the vision of the mind's hundreds of eyes continues for an imagination no longer trapped by the seasons.

Stevens ends his poem with the mind's eyes poised at reality's advancing wave-crest prepared to uncover new forms. He describes his cantos as "the edgings and inchings of final form, /

The swarming activities of the formulae" (CP 488). Realizing
that the "said words of the world are the life of the world" (CP
474), he traces the minutiae of creation—the "Flickings from
finikin to fine finikin" (CP 488)—and evolves through word forms
imitating the mind's life "urgent proof that the theory / Of poetry
is the theory of life" (CP 486). He accepts James's maxim that
"the only escape is by the practical way" (WB 604) and refuses
old age's hollow luxury of releasing the imagination's grip on the
pragmatic world. "The marvel is," writes Brown, "that in such
fidelity to common life, Stevens was able to articulate such magnificence."[26] For the pragmatist, the common life contains all the
magnificence the mind can know, and Stevens rejects none of it.

James proposes in his essays on pragmatism a clarifying context
for understanding both the substance and the form of "An Ordinary Evening in New Haven":

it seems a grudging and sickly way of meeting so robust a universe to
shrink from any of its facts and wish them not to be. Rather take the
strictly dramatic point of view, and treat the whole thing as a great
unending romance which the spirit of the universe, striving to realize
its own content, is eternally thinking out and representing to itself.
(WB 602)

In the great, unending poem of "things seen and unseen, created
from nothingness" (CP 486), Stevens' spirit of imagination eternally thinks out and represents to itself the particulars of the
robust universe. Through making poems from the immediacy of
perception, the imagination realizes its own content and its own
form. More than this, at the edge of nothingness, it realizes its
own contentment in perpetuating forward movement. The incon-
venience of winter does not "menace" the visions of "An Ordinary Evening," as Bloom suggests.[27] Stevens knows that "It is not
in the premise that reality / Is a solid" (CP 489), that winter
presents not an end but yet another landscape of the flux to
which the mind must attune itself. In the poems of The Rock,
his final collection, Stevens continues the process of attunement
and of making the last years of his imaginative life as vital as any
other. "I have never been bored in any general sense," Stevens

once wrote, "and at my ripe age, I am quite sure that I never shall be" (LWS 533). The vitality of life at whatever age issues from the mind's power to create poems that "stimulate some sense of living and of being alive" (OP 177). Living in a pluralism, Stevens embraces all of the implications of multiplicity:

> And these images, these reverberations,
> And others, make certain how being
> Includes death and the imagination.

(CP 444)

5 TOWARD STILLNESS

The Rock

tevens' last poems enact a fulfillment of the earlier explorations of poetry as a process of evolving fictive certainties. The final and shortest section of *The Collected Poems, The Rock* manifests a poet able to affirm in the shadow of personal annihilation the continuing vitality of the imagination. The imminence of physical return to the earth-mother and to the rock as generative source of both physical and imaginative life prompts Stevens to adjust his late style from the impersonal tone of the meditations in "The Auroras of Autumn" to poems asserting the primacy of personal and individual experience. "The section, seen as a unit," Riddel writes, "is a carefully planned farewell."[1] Preparing to leave the world, Stevens returns wholeheartedly to its particulars and fashions a farewell consistent to his lifelong commitment to the actual and to the sacred power of the imagination to supply meaning to an otherwise meaningless void. While it represents a visionary and metaphysical distillation, Stevens' rock issues directly from the physical, for reality is the secular temple of the imagination's redeeming power.

Acting as poet-priest of the earth's holiness, in *The Rock* Stevens advances the lineaments of the Emersonian scholar-self toward apotheosis. His pervasive interest in the central-perceiving self and its derivation intensifies, a fascination he showed in a practical way by hiring a genealogist in the early forties to trace his ancestry. Holly Stevens reports that, during a ten year period ending in 1952, over four hundred letters were written to various professional people—including several pastors of country churches in eastern Pennsylvania—concerning genealogical matters. To Hi

Simons, Stevens exclaimed that "the whole thing has been an extraordinary experience: finding out about my family, etc. It is extraordinary how little seems to have survived when you first begin to study this sort of thing and then later on, when you have learned how to go about it, what an immense amount has survived and how much you can make of it" (LWS 457). Another letter discloses that "the family picture is like a good many other pictures of a different sort. There seems to be a tremendous thickness of varnish of a more or less romantic sort all over the thing, and I want to take that all off and get down to the real people" (LWS 499). Enacting his familiar pattern of decreating to get to the real, Stevens' intent is to "try to let a little daylight into the attic of the past" (LWS 448) and more specifically to analyze ancestral branches in order to "determine whether I fit into the line, and how" (LWS 448).

More than idle historical curiosity, Stevens' foray into the roots of his heritage indicates a concern for the origins and sources of the self. He wishes to construe the poetic self in the facticity of its proper milieu and to transfer the fertile particulars of his origins into the imagination's life. Having arrived in "Final Soliloquy of the Interior Paramour" at what Riddel calls "the ultimate discovery of his aesthetic"[2]—the realization that "God and the imagination are one" (CP 524), Stevens seeks a finite and empirical source for the God-encompassing self to replace the hollow heaven occupied by the impersonal God of myth. If God and mind are one and the mind's proper place is within a physical world, then reality constitutes the only possible heaven. The poet's genealogical chart therefore begins at reality's generative center. Stevens clarifies this heritage in "The Irish Cliffs of Moher":

> Who is my father in this world, in this house,
> At the spirit's base?
>
> My father's father, his father's father, his—
> Shadows like winds
>
> Go back to a parent before thought, before speech,
> At the head of the past.

> They go to the cliffs of Moher rising out of the mist,
> Above the real,
>
> Rising out of present time and place, . . .
>
>   .   .   .   .
> .,. . This is my father, or, maybe,
> It is as he was,
>
> A likeness, one of the race of fathers: earth
> And sea and air.
>
>   (CP 501–2)

Another variation on the rock, the cliffs of Moher represent the core of all creation. They derive from the same figure Stevens had used in "Credences of Summer" to denote the essential barrenness—"the natural tower of all the world" and the "mountain on which the tower stands" (CP 373). What in "Credences" was the "final mountain" and "point of survey" now stands as a point of nascency and a wellspring of poetic activity. The old man on the tower who in the earlier poem represented regeneration evolves into the more specific figure of the primitive earth as "parent before thought," the vital father progenitor of all imaginative power.

As an aging man tracing his lineage both literally and poetically, Stevens' concern is to conceive the self in its *wholeness* within a concrete and sacred physical universe. He once wrote to his niece concerning his father that "seeing him as a whole, I understand him better perhaps than he understood himself. . . . I can really look into his heart in which he must have concealed so many things" (LWS 458). All of Stevens' fathers, figurative and real, contribute to the whole self his poems strive to define. In "Prologues to What Is Possible," he provides a fuller explanation of the relationship between heredity, self-definition and poetry:

> What self, for example, did he contain that had not
>   yet been loosed,
> Snarling in him for discovery as his attentions spread,
> As if all his hereditary lights were suddenly increased.
>
>   (CP 516–17)

By spreading his attention toward more and more particulars within life's flux, including the particulars of his own heritage, Stevens releases newer selves snarling for discovery in the form of poems as acts of self-creation. His "hereditary" lights consist of individual "smallest lamp[s]" of imaginative insight. Each adds "its puissant flick" as the poet's mind supplies "A name and privilege over the ordinary of his commonplace" (CP 517). Meditating upon the world, the mind creates a fresh version of the self and adds another branch to the familial tree. Nearing the end of life, Stevens desires that no selves be trapped by a failure of vision. Instead, his mind continues its ceaseless activity as each "flick" contributes to what is real and "Creates a fresh universe out of nothingness by adding itself" (CP 517). This process insures the continuing freshness of self and world alike.

Not surprisingly, since Stevens' investigations of self-origin repeat the emphases of "The American Scholar" and "Self-Reliance," he finally confronts squarely his ancestral lines to Emerson. "Looking Across the Fields and Watching the Birds Fly" discusses the fundamental differences between the scholar's guise of Emerson (spoken of as a clownish "Mr. Homburg") and a similar role for the contemporary poet. Stevens opens the poem in a tone of unmistakable mockery of his literary forefather:

> Among the more irritating minor ideas
> Of Mr. Homburg during his visits home
> To Concord, at the edge of things, was this:
>
> To think away the grass, the trees, the clouds,
> Not to transform them into other things,
> Is only what the sun does every day.
>
> (CP 517)

At the edge and not at the center, Mr. Homburg's quest for the first idea is not "flicked by feeling" (CP 407). He becomes all mind and devises a "slightly detestable *operandum*," by which Stevens implies transcendentalism: "No doubt we live beyond ourselves in air" (CP 518). Reflecting upon Emerson's philosophy, Stevens christens himself "A new scholar replacing an older one" (CP 519). His office is to seek "For a human that can be accounted for" (CP 519) to replace "the masculine myths we used to make" (CP 518). Very subtly, the tone of mockery switches to a tone of high seriousness as Stevens realizes that if Emerson's transcendental, philosophical base missed the proper mode for the man of imagination, it caught nevertheless the essential spirit that issues from processive living:

> What we know in what we see, what we feel in what
> We hear, what we are, beyond mystic disputation,
> In the tumult of integrations out of the sky,
>
> And what we think, a breathing like the wind,
> A moving part of a motion, a discovery
> Part of a discovery, a change part of a change,
>
> . . . .
>
> A daily majesty of meditation.
>
> (CP 518)

Through willing acceptance of the mantle of the modern "American Scholar," Stevens declares his affinity to the heritage of the American self extending directly from Emerson through Thoreau and Whitman to himself. Rejecting Mr. Homburg's intellective pomposity, Stevens accepts his imaginative vision. The new scholar must replace the central self as hero with the central self as human and must assume a greater responsibility of self-reliance than Emerson embraced in an era still protected by "masculine myths." Stevens indicates his acceptance of Emerson's concept of the relationship between mind and nature. The imagination responds to the "blunt laws" (CP 519) of the natural world and forms itself as a contrary power issuing from the same source:

> The spirit comes from the body of the world,
> Or so Mr. Homburg thought: the body of a world
> Whose blunt laws make an affectation of mind,
>
> The mannerism of nature caught in a glass
> And there become a spirit's mannerism,
> A glass aswarm with things going as far as they can.
>
> (CP 519)

Meditating the world, the glass or mirror of imagination reflects the world's mannerism, which in the process of creative transposition becomes its own. Another richly multifarious image, Stevens' "glass" is the last of several direct allusions occurring throughout *The Collected Poems* to Emerson's "transparent eyeball." For Emerson, the eye was "the best of artists" as well as the "best composer" because "by the mutual action of its structure" it could integrate dissimilar objects of whatever kind "into a well-colored and shaded globe" and produce symmetry and perspective (CWE I 15). Aswarm with reality, Stevens' eye of imagination reconstitutes what it perceives within the form of its own container—the poem itself, the final variation on the image of the glass. Perspective comes then from the glass of imagination—the perceiving eye —filtering reality through its colors and shades and producing the glass as poem—container for the richness of the world.

Stevens consummates his investigation into the sources of the self in "The Sail of Ulysses," a poem written less than two years before his death. In this piece his allusions to Emerson are less overt than in "Looking Across the Fields and Watching the Birds Fly" but the delineations of an Emersonian scholar-self in modern posture are unmistakable. Where Emerson had described the scholar as "Man Thinking," Stevens defines the "true creator" or poet as "the thinker / Thinking gold thoughts in a golden mind" (OP 100). Where Emerson's scholar plied "the slow, unhonored, and unpaid task of observation" (CWE I 100), Stevens' thinker partakes of

> a human loneliness,
> A part of space and solitude,
>
> . . . . .
> In which nothing of knowledge fails.
>
> (OP 100)

Finally, where the office of Emerson's scholar was "to cheer, to raise, and to guide men by showing them facts amidst appearances" (CWE I 100), Stevens' true creator, "creating from nothingness" in a world without teleology, discovers "The joy of meaning in design / Wrenched out of chaos" (OP 100). In each case,

Stevens' scholar continues the tradition Emerson established of a thinking man, unhonored in his genius, who discovers the world for mankind.

Ulysses becomes for Stevens a figure for the self en route. In separate places he refers to him as "The interminable adventurer" (CP 520) and "Symbol of the seeker" (OP 99). Ever so carefully in "The Sail of Ulysses" Stevens elaborates a justification of the ways not of God but of self to man. In a pluralism "There is no map of paradise" and "the genealogy / Of gods and men" (OP 102) are rightfully destroyed as man approaches generative vision:

> The ancient symbols will be nothing then.
> We shall have gone behind the symbols
> To that which they symbolized.
>
> (OP 102)

Stevens repeats a lifelong emphasis that the awesome burden weighing upon the central self in a universe devoid of symbols is to be "Master of the world and of himself" (OP 102):

> His mind presents the world
> And in his mind the world revolves.
>
> . . . .
>
> Like things produced by a climate, the world
> Goes round in the climates of the mind
> And bears its floraisons of imagery.
>
> (OP 102)

Here Stevens makes his clearest statement concerning the imagination's metaphorical counterpart to the temporal flow of the seasons discovered in "Credences of Summer." As each alteration of climate produces the characteristic changes that define spring, summer, autumn, and winter, so in the seasons of the mind, parallel to but separate from literal time, the world changes according to the imagination's perception of it within the "floraisons of imagery." The infinite variety of the self specifies the infinite variety of the world. Since "the world goes round and round / In the crystal atmospheres of the mind" (OP 102), reality unfolds only within the scope of each individual's experience of it. This is what Emerson realized when he wrote that "to believe your own thought . . . is genius" and insisted that man must learn to detect "that gleam of light which flashes across his mind from within" (CWE II 45). For Stevens and Emerson both, freedom consists in the release of man from the intimidation of other minds and in the cultivation of the powers of his own. "How then shall the mind be less than free," Stevens asks, "Since only to know is to be free" (OP 103).

Once the self attains the freedom of self-knowledge, Stevens predicts a culmination, within process, of Emerson's thinking man:

> The center of the self, the self
> Of the future, of future man
> And future place, when these are known,
> A freedom at last from the mystical,
> The beginning of a final order,
> The order of man's right to be
> As he is, the discipline of his scope
> Observed as an absolute, himself.
>
> (OP 101)

The "final order" achieved by the central self has nothing to do with fixity or system but involves simply the free activity of a regenerative imagination within the flux of space and solitude. In the twilight of his own selfhood, this is the order Stevens hopes to have achieved. His quest for a genealogy of the self ends in the realization that

> In the generations of thought, man's sons
> And heirs are powers of the mind,
> His only testament and estate.
>
> (OP 103)

Knowing he will soon die, his search constitutes an effort to solidify before his departure the consummate relevance of the creative self in the nonteleological world. He expresses this effort clearly in "Note on Moonlight":

> The one moonlight, the various universe, intended
> So much just to be seen—a purpose, empty
> Perhaps, absurd perhaps, but at least a purpose,
> Certain and ever more fresh. Ah! Certain, for sure . . .
>
> (CP 532)

Here Stevens reflects upon the glory of certitude in a universe of uncertainty. The single imagination ("one moonlight") perceives the many ("various universe") and in that act fulfills itself. That a mind standing on the edge of nothingness continues to discover fresh visions of the world, as Stevens does in his final poems, attests to the ultimate peace and freedom the self can achieve amid chaos.

Frank Doggett notices that in "The Sail of Ulysses" Stevens "presents all the infinite abstraction of time and space, all of reality, as depending upon the most particular form of being, the 'moment of light,' the instant of experience in one individual mind."[3] The specific passage to which Doggett refers combines in an exquisite manner the essence of James's pragmatic theory:

> The living man in the present place,
> Always, the particular thought
> Among Plantagenet abstractions,
> Always and always, the difficult inch,
> On which the vast arches of space
> Repose, always, the credible thought
> From which the incredible systems spring
>
> . . . .
> . . . these
> Are the manifestations of a law
> That bends the particulars to the abstract,
>
> . . . .
> As if abstractions were, themselves
> Particulars of a relative sublime.
>
> (OP 103)

As James realized, "no one can live an hour without both facts and principles" (PR 364). Stevens demonstrates that the source of principles, abstractions and sublimities rests always within a single mind's particular thought. Incredible systems evolve from the activity of a central imagination responding within each difficult inch of a processive existence to the specifics of its world. Since empiricism means *"the habit of explaining wholes by parts"* (PU 484), Stevens resists to the end the temptation toward the opposing course of explaining parts by wholes. Where the former option renders man the center and originator of Plantagenet abstractions, the latter positions him on the periphery of existence, where his present place is insignificant and where Plantagenet abstractions overwhelm him. What follows is James's prose equivalent of Stevens' passage:

For pluralism, all that we are required to admit as the constitution of reality is what we ourselves find empirically realized in every minimum of finite life. Briefly it is this, that nothing real is absolutely simple, that every smallest bit of experience is a *multum in parvo* plurally related, that each relation is one aspect, character, or function, way of its being taken, or way of its taking something else; and that a bit of reality when actively engaged in one of these relations is not *by that very fact* engaged in all the other relations simultaneously. (PU 807)

James's "every minimum of finite life" becomes Stevens' "difficult inch" of "particular thought." Every self must "find empirically realized" a reality stripped of conceptualization and emanating not from the "vast arches of space" but from "every smallest bit of experience." Stevens elaborates in "The Sail of Ulysses" a self whose present moment in the actual world defines both self and world. As he wrote in the *Adagia*, "The world is myself. Life is myself" (OP 172). In his late poetry, he affirms that life's fullness does not wane in life's passing and that the mind's freedom is not diminished by death's presence.

Other than the title poem itself, Stevens' highest poetic achievement in *The Rock* is "To an Old Philosopher in Rome," written on the occasion of George Santayana's death in 1952. The life and person of Santayana provided Stevens an emblem of the emancipated self in the modern world and an appropriately solemn twentieth-century substitute for "Mr. Homburg." While a Harvard student, Stevens had been invited to Santayana's home in Cambridge to read poems to him. Forty years later, he recalls that "I always came away from my visits to him feeling that he made up in the most genuine way for many things that I needed" (LWS 482). When Santayana died in a Roman Catholic convent, Stevens recorded his grief in a letter to Barbara Church referring to him as "a man whose whole life is thought" (LWS 761). Facing his own death, Stevens strongly identifies with one who lived the life of the mind and who found, like himself, abiding consolation in a materialistic and nonteleological universe. "It is one of the great human paradoxes," Riddel proposes, "that the masses of our contemporary world refuse to be lonely and are, while Santayana chose to be lonely and was not."[4] "To an Old Philosopher in Rome" affirms with exquisite restraint the pleasure-pain extremes of pragmatic existence James continually described.

Stevens reemphasizes in the poem that the "celestial possible" exists in the actual, in the "last drop of the deepest blood" (CP 509). "On the threshold of heaven" (CP 508), Santayana lies on his deathbed and catches within glimpses of flickering consciousness the spectacle of a religious street procession. The meditation assumes the perspective of the dying man's imagination. On the point of death, Santayana's life of the mind does not falter. He transmutes the figures in the street parade into a vision of heavenly movement—"the majestic movement / Of men growing small in the distances of space" (CP 508). Himself growing smaller and smaller in the vicissitudes of living, the old philosopher has regressed to a mere "shadow of a shape / In a confusion on bed" (CP 509). He is a pitiable remnant of man who for consolation must "speak to [his] pillow as if it was [himself]" and who can locate the grandeur he deserves only "In so much misery" (CP 509).

Nowhere else in his poetry does Stevens portray the heroic self in such absolutely diminutive circumstance. Santayana's predicament becomes a metaphor for the point Stevens has reached in his own imaginative situation when the imminence of death renders life "A light on the candle tearing against the wick" (CP 509). The poem celebrates, however, not the defeat but the apotheosis of the dying self. Externally miserable and pathetic, Santayana maintains the internal vitality that characterized his entire life. From the particulars of the holy city of Rome he fashions in the imagination a portrait of that "merciful Rome / Beyond, the two alike in the make of the mind" (CP 508). The process of the mind's uninterrupted *making* converts the human city into an otherwise unachievable heavenly city:

> It is as if in a human dignity
> Two parallels become one, a perspective, of which
> Men are part both in the inch and in the mile.
>
> (CP 508)

As Brown notes, parallels cannot touch except in the "miracle of old age on the verge of death that is the basis of the whole poem."[5] The perspective Santayana achieves emanates from the conjuncture of "The extreme of the known in the presence of the extreme / Of the unknown" (CP 508). The "extreme of the known" is the dying man's experience of its own death-moment— the final knowing at the end of knowing. The "extreme of the unknown" suggests man's maximum ignorance of the state he inherits once death's moment has passed. The peace of perspective issues then from the expiring philosopher's ability to fuse the parallels of two extremes—represented by actual Rome and the Rome beyond—within the act of the mind. Since the mind's activity forms both the real world and the world of heavenly vision, man can partake of the centrality of existence—"both in the inch and in the mile"—up to his final breath.

Part of the greatness of "To an Old Philosopher in Rome" derives from Stevens' unrelenting attention to the concrete detail of the death-scene. If it constitutes a poverty for man not to *live* in a physical world, as Stevens previously established, he indicates here as great a poverty not to *die* in one. As Santayana lies "dozing in the depths of wakefulness" (CP 509), the particulars of his immediate surroundings feed and shape his celestial vision. The banners in the religious procession convert to angels' wings, the medicinal smells of the sickroom become "A fragrantness not to be spoiled" (CP 508) and the "newsboys' muttering" outside the window transforms into a spiritual "murmuring" within the mind. Stevens illustrates the Jamesian premise that the edifice of the mind must always comprise the architecture of the empirical world:

> The sounds drift in. The buildings are remembered.
> The life of the city never lets go, nor do you
> Ever want it to. It is part of the life in your room.
> Its domes are the architecture of your bed.
>   . . . .
> It is a kind of total grandeur at the end,
> With every visible thing enlarged and yet
> No more than a bed, a chair and moving nuns,
> The immensest theatre, the pillared porch,
> The book and candle in your ambered room.
>
> (CP 510)

On his deathbed, Santayana experiences the heaven-in-earth that constitutes the only possible paradise. His "total grandeur" remains inseparable from the poverty of his end because while the imagination enlarges upon reality it does not eliminate any of its particulars. It raises them, however, to the level of the sacred and locates the seat of holiness in the minutiae of daily living. By elevating the details of the city that never lets go to the level of a spiritual vision, Santayana's secular imagination redeems itself in the precise instant of its demise. Stevens cannot help but identify and admire:

> So that we feel, in this illumined large,
> The veritable small, so that each of us
> Beholds himself in you, and hears his voice
> In yours, master and commiserable man,
> Intent on your particles of nether-do.
>
> (CP 509)

Stevens realizes that each man's life dissolves to the same lonely room. He clarifies in "Lebensweisheitspielerei" that the only persons left in "the poverty / Of autumnal space" are:

> The finally human,
> Natives of a dwindled sphere.

> . . . .
> Each person completely touches us
> With what he is and as he is,
> In the stale grandeur of annihilation.
>
> (CP 504–5)

In these natives may be found the essence of mankind, what James refers to as "human nature *in extremis* . . . strained to its uttermost and on the rack . . . the reality of which it seems to be the function of all the higher forms of literature and fine art to bring home to us and suggest" (TT 648).

Stevens saw in George Santayana an emblem of human nature in extremis, a man whose life of the mind in "the afflatus of ruin" was so fully lived it made him "The one invulnerable man among / Crude captains, the naked majesty, if you like" (CP 510). Santayana knows that the heaven is actually the ground of earth: "He stops upon this threshold" (CP 511). There is no need to go on. After all, every heavenly city the mind has fashioned traces its genesis to the particulars of the here and now. The pluralistic universe therefore is sufficient to sustain the imagination's final puissant flick.

Like Santayana, Stevens confronts his end without remorse. Withering into winter, he accepts the final season when "It is as if / We had come to an end of the imagination" (CP 502). Even in this awareness, when the "great structure" of the mind "has become a minor house" and it seems "A fantastic effort has failed" (CP 502), mere consciousness implies life's vibrancy:

> Yet the absence of the imagination had
> Itself to be imagined. The great pond,
> The plain sense of it, without reflections, leaves,
>
> . . . .
> . . . all this
> Had to be imagined as an inevitable knowledge,
> Required, as a necessity requires.
>
> (CP 503)

Because it is an imaginative act, the mind's contemplation of its own annihilation and the scenery of its own nothingness carries forward the secular redemption implicit in the power of poetry.

In these late poems, Stevens no longer questions as he had done earlier the suitability of language to express the mind's visions. Where the man with his blue guitar complained at the ineffi- ciency of his instrument to "play things as they are" and con- cluded "I cannot bring a world quite round, / Although I patch it as I can" (CP 165), the older Stevens discovers words are not semantic structures that impede the work of the imagination; they *do* bring the world round and fully participate in the process of mind confronting reality. In "Prologues to What Is Possible," he dramatizes the resilience of the mind-language relationship. The poem opens with a simple simile: "There was an ease of mind that was like being alone in a boat at sea" (CP 515). In its quest to define its own well-being, the imagination elaborates a complex fiction involving ocean waves, the bright backs of rowers, the grip- ping of oars. During the process of pursuing words to express itself, the mind goes beyond the scope of its original intent and arrives at the point of the first idea almost in spite of itself:

> As he traveled alone, like a man lured on by a syllable without any
>   meaning,
> A syllable of which he felt, with an appointed sureness,
> That it contained the meaning into which he wanted to enter,
> A meaning which, as he entered it, would shatter the boat and
>   leave the oarsmen quiet
> As at a point of central arrival, an instant moment, much or little,
> Removed from any shore, from any man or woman, and needing
>   none.
>
>   (CP 516)

Like all processes, the activity of generating fictive structures leads the mind in unpredictable directions. The very effort of writing the poem, of pursuing syllables to describe the "ease of mind," leads to a central vision, the highest accomplishment of the poetic act. By joining perception to vocabulary, the poet achieves more than he bargained for: "The metaphor stirred his fear. The object with which he was compared / Was beyond his recognizing" (CP

516). The certainty of his fiction unsettles him because he realizes he has uncovered a new aspect of the self that he did not know was there, and that the lure of syllables will result in other metaphors equally profound and unsettling. Stevens indicates that the poet's approximations do more than "patch" reality. They uncover and reveal it. The imagination's realm involves "The loftiest syllables among loftiest things" (CP 510). The poet's words among the world's particulars constitute an earthly spirituality to replace what used to be "loftiest" heaven.

That which is revealed, always, is the holiness of the rock. In the title piece of his final collection, Stevens culminates his lifelong assertion of the sacred foundation of empirical living and the spiritual office of the poet's role as secular priest. "The Rock" fulfills both Emerson's notion of the universe as a wondrous visionary place and James's belief in the power of man's mind to engender truth upon reality. Stevens enacts in this holiest of poems a major assimilation and revaluation of his theory in order to discover what he refers to as the "cure" and "ground" of self and world. As Ronald Sukenick suggests, the rock represents "that base of man's life out of which he grows and from which he descends in death."[6] At once birthstone and gravestone, Stevens' "synthetic"[7] rock embodies a merging of all contraries—beginning and end, imagination and reality, permanence and impermanence. All become one in the "ground" of the mind of man.

Yet, if Stevens' poem attempts an assimilation, this does not imply a sterile reiteration of earlier premises. In the first canto of "The Rock," subtitled "Seventy Years Later," Stevens expunges all of the old fictive houses in which the imagination sheltered itself:

> It is an illusion that we were ever alive,
> Lived in the houses of mothers, arranged ourselves
> By our own motions in a freedom of air.
>
> Regard the freedom of seventy years ago.
> It is no longer air. The houses still stand,
> Though they are rigid in rigid emptiness.

> Even our shadows, their shadows, no longer remain.
> The lives these lived in the mind are at an end.
> They never were . . .
>
> (CP 525)

An aspect of process, freedom cannot be defined in past moments of vitality. Stevens restates the Emersonian premise that "your action is good only whilst it is alive,—whilst it is in you" (EJ VII 202). The freedom of seventy years ago is an illusion because it no longer lives but comprises the stale fixity of the remembered past. Stevens refuses to lapse into the now hollow comforts of a vibrant yesterday. He rejects the postulates of old poems such as those in "The Man with the Blue Guitar": "The sounds of the guitar / Were not and are not. Absurd" (CP 525). Seventy years later, the poet's freedom issues as always from a heroic response to present particulars.

If Stevens rejects the mind's old forms, he does not disparage them, for they were original acts of perception as much as this present poem and emanated from the same decreation-creation process. Each past poem embodied

> an illusion so desired
> That the green leaves came and covered the high rock,
> That the lilacs came and bloomed, like a blindness cleaned.
>
> (CP 526)

The mind's desire to cover the rock with the leaves and lilacs of its fictions must never be quenched because the poet's "vital assumption" of the nature of existence is that it consists of "an impermanence / In its permanent cold" (CP 526). Himself about to become the victim of impermanence, Stevens' last poetic acts continue to affirm the fundamental pragmatic contention that change vitalizes life:

> The blooming and the musk
> Were being alive, an incessant being alive,
> A particular of being, that gross universe.
>
> (CP 526)

The poet fixes the rock in foliage. The leaves wither to illusion. The poet returns to the "particular," fecund, and voluptuous ("gross") universe and repeats the same process endlessly.

But the mere repetition of the process seems not enough. In the second canto, "The Poem as Icon," Stevens raises the poet's poems or "leaves" to the level of sacramental objects:

> It is not enough to cover the rock with leaves.
> We must be cured of it by a cure of the ground
> Or a cure of ourselves, that is equal to a cure
>
> Of the ground, a cure beyond forgetfulness.

> (CP 526)

If the imagination simply covers the rock with leaves and imitates nature's birth-death cyclicity, it cannot escape nature's violence. The poem saves or "cures" man of the rock's violence by metaphorically redeeming him in the imagination's time scheme. The poet discovers a "cure of ourselves . . . equal to a cure / Of the ground" within the energy of each fictive act. The "ground" is the empirical world. In this poem, Stevens brings the ground of reality totally within the landscape of the imagination. External and internal grounds become one in the central mind.

As an image of sacred reality, the poem as icon participates in a secular spirituality parallel to the Christian myth of the Eucharist, in which a blessed host (the icon of Christ) is consumed and a worshiper is temporarily redeemed or cured. Stevens' imagery invokes a similar ritual:

> And yet the leaves, if they broke into bud,
> If they broke into bloom, if they bore fruit,
>
> And if we ate the incipient colorings
> Of their fresh culls might be a cure of the ground.
> The fiction of the leaves is the icon
>
> Of the poem, the figuration of blessedness,
> And the icon is the man.

> (CP 526)

Stevens carefully constructs his religious parallel around "if." In fact, the poet does not consume his own sanctifying fictions, but since his poems unite him with nature's vitality (as the communion host unites the Christian with the vital Christ) and redeem him from insignificance, fixity, and cyclical death, they constitute "figuration[s] of blessedness" in a secular universe. Through his fictions, the poet adds "New senses in the engenderings of sense" (CP 527) by specifying reality's rich core—"The honey in its pulp, the final found, / The plenty of the year and of the world" (CP 527). Most important, in covering the barren rock with leaves, the priest-poet supplies meaning to a meaningless void and eliminates the barrenness within each creative act:

> In this plenty, the poem makes meanings of the rock,
> Of such mixed motion and such imagery
> That its barrenness becomes a thousand things
>
> And so exists no more. This is the cure
> Of leaves and of the ground and of ourselves.
> His words are both the icon and the man.
>
> (CP 527)

Poem, poet and world participate equally in the secular holiness. "The Rock" substantiates what Stevens meant when he wrote in the *Adagia:* "After one has abandoned a belief in god, poetry is that essence which takes its place as life's redemption" (OP 158).

The ultimate statement of poetry's redemptive power comes in the final canto, "Forms of the Rock in a Night-Hymn." Stevens examines the rock's essential barrenness from the point of view of one about to die, and still finds it man's rightful home, the only paradise to which he should aspire. He avoids sentimentalizing the rock's awesome significance:

> The rock is the gray particular of man's life,
> The stone from which he rises, up—and—ho,
> The step to the bleaker depths of his descents . . .
>
> The rock is the stern particular of the air.
>
> (CP 528)

Stern and inescapable, the rock proclaims man's birth and man's doom. Infinitely larger than man, it is a "mirror of the planets," the "habitation of the whole" (CP 528). Yet the poet renders the rock man's own through his ability to compose night hymns, such as this one, that imbue reality with the only meaning it can possess. In Riddel's words, "the rock as both origin and end of self is discovered to have its own origin and end in the self."[8] Subsuming the world into the horizons of the eye of imagination (the "silent rhapsodist"), the poet celebrates the rock instead of fearing it and discovers peace within the holiness of his fictions:

> It is the rock where tranquil must adduce
> Its tranquil self, the main of things, the mind,
>
> The starting point of the human and the end,
> That in which space itself is contained.
>
> (CP 528)

Stevens ends his poetic quest at the beginning, with the mind's eye as the first circle in a universe of flowing particulars. There is nothing surprising or contradictory in Stevens' high religious sentiment at the conclusion of his life. James reveals that the pragmatist need not be divorced from religion. "I myself invincibly do believe," he writes, "that, although all the special manifestations of religion may have been absurd (I mean its creeds and theories), yet the life of it as a whole is mankind's most important function" (LWJ II 127). Stevens writes poetry as a religious act and proposes his poems as sacred replacements for sterile doctrinal creeds and theories. The poet's function, revealed in "The Rock," is to illumine reality within fictive hymns that vitalize the self by renewing the world. The poet's imaginative visions forever return him to the "starting point," the point of "Naked Alpha" (CP 469) where self and world are incessantly renewed.

Stevens closes his collection on the threshold of new life. The final poem, "Not Ideas About the Thing But the Thing Itself," takes the imagination out of winter and away from death into still another spring:

> At the earliest ending of winter,
> In March, a scrawny cry from outside
> Seemed like a sound in his mind.
>
> (CP 534)

Vendler errs in finding this a poem of death in which "old age . . . is in fact inhabiting a pre-history, as the soul, not yet born, waits to be reincarnated."[9] Life, not death, reincarnates Stevens' imagination. This is a poem of beginnings, not ends. The "scrawny cry" is a bird's song "In the early March wind" announcing the advent of another cyclical phase: "He knew that he heard it, / A bird's cry, at daylight or before" (CP 534). Hardly a "November voice" that "cannot even articulate itself into verse,"[10] Stevens' voice of old age is clear and celebrational. A new season for the imagination's life has begun, and the mind leaps at the faraway sound that hints it is time to discard winter's fictions and dress itself anew in reality's forms. "The sun was coming from outside" (CP 534)—not the mind's inside idea of sun, but a new sun, a spring reality, leafless, which the imagination again must fix in foliage. Stevens' last piece indicates the imagination redeemed once more and poised in splendid anticipation:

> That scrawny cry—it was
> A chorister whose c preceded the choir.
> It was part of the colossal sun,
>
> Surrounded by its choral rings,
> Still far away. It was like
> A new knowledge of reality.
>
> (CP 534)

Considered as an aspect of intellectual history outside the lines of direct influence, the varieties of imagination represented in Emerson, James, and Stevens signify a clear tradition in the development of the American self. Stevens brings forward into a nihilistic age the Emersonian scholar-self whose mode was affirmation, discovery, and freedom. From James's philosophy of practicality, he advances the notion of man engendering his own truths upon a universe evolving through an endless procession of facts. He projects that "the final poem will be the poem of fact in the language of fact" (OP 164). From Emerson's transcendental idealism, he fulfills the notion of the vitality of thought and of change in a visionary world. The difficult synthesis of idealism and practicality specifies Stevens' unique genius and his special relevance to a demythologized era characterized by depression and ennui. Like James and Emerson before him, whose theories permeate his entire canon, Stevens liberates the mind from arid abstraction and fixity by devising a philosophy and a poetry that is "present perfecting" (OP 167).

The liberation was gradual. The growth of Stevens' poetry from *Harmonium* to *The Rock* follows the Emersonian lines of a poetic self, initially tentative and inconsistent in its creative voice, advancing with increasing confidence into the center of the life of the mind. In a world without gods and lacking any teleological base, Stevens' challenge to himself was "to find the spiritual in reality" (OP 178) and to "establish aesthetics in the individual mind as immeasurably a greater thing than religion" (OP 166). The foundation of this aesthetic is that "the mind is the most powerful thing in the world" (OP 162) and that it creates from the energy of original insight the necessary and exquisite fictions on which modern man, if he is to survive the death of the gods, must sustain himself. With heaven and hell destroyed, Stevens focuses the attention of his imagination on the ground of earth, the particulars of a world caught in the permanence of ceaseless change. He realizes evil as inseparable from process; by assimilating evil into his aesthetic, he frees himself from transempirical dependence and arrives at a point where the imagination begins redeeming itself by its own generative visions. Hence, the imagination recovers in the rock of an empirical world the heaven it thought it had lost. Stevens learns that "the mind that in heaven created the earth and the mind that on earth created heaven were, as it happened, one" (OP 176). Both, that is, were the mind of man. In the secular and vibrant temple of his present reality, Stevens creates redeeming songs that "renew the world in a verse" (OP 103) and delight in the facticity of mere being.

NOTES

Chapter 1: *Advance on Chaos and the Dark*

[1] The titles of works by Emerson, James, and Stevens are abbreviated in page references throughout this book. A complete list of those abbreviations precedes the preface.

[2] Frederic I. Carpenter, "William James and Emerson," *American Literature*, 11 (1939), 39.

[3] Eduard C. Lindeman, "Emerson's Pragmatic Mood," *American Scholar*, 16 (1946–47), 57–64.

[4] Margaret L. W. Peterson, "*Harmonium* and William James," *Southern Review*, 7 (1971), 659.

[5] James E. Mulqueen, "Wallace Stevens: Radical Transcendentalist," *Midwest Quarterly*, 11 (1970), 329–40.

[6] Frank Doggett, *Stevens' Poetry of Thought* (Baltimore, Md.: Johns Hopkins University Press, 1966), p. 19.

[7] Harold Bloom, *Wallace Stevens: The Poems of Our Climate* (Ithaca, N.Y.: Cornell University Press, 1976), p. 10.

[8] Carpenter alludes to this in "William James and Emerson," p. 50.

[9] Morse Peckham, "An Introduction to Emerson's Essays [1968]" in *Romanticism and Behavior* (Columbia: University of South Carolina Press, 1976), p. 131.

[10] John J. McDermott, Introduction to *The Writings of William James: A Comprehensive Edition* (Chicago: University of Chicago Press, 1977), p. xxxv.

[11] McDermott, p. 448. McDermott takes this comment from Ralph Barton Perry's *The Thought and Character of William James*, 2 vols. combined (Boston: Little, Brown, 1935), pp. 478–80. Perry, in turn, notes that the comment came originally from James's manuscripts and then appeared in Edwin Bjorkman's interview with James in the *New York Times*, November 3, 1907.

[12] Morse Peckham, *Man's Rage for Chaos: Biology, Behavior and the Arts* (Philadelphia: Chilton, 1965), p. xi.

[13] Harold Bloom, "The Central Man: Emerson, Whitman, Wallace Stevens," *Massachusetts Review*, 7 (1966), 42.

[14] Roy Harvey Pearce, *The Continuity of American Poetry* (Princeton, N.J.: Princeton University Press, 1961), p. 392.

[15] Edwin Arlington Robinson, "The Man Against the Sky," in *The American Tradition in Literature*, ed. Sculley Bradley, et al. (New York: W. W. Norton, 1974), p. 881.

[16] Joseph Riddel, *The Clairvoyant Eye: The Poetry and Poetics of Wallace Stevens* (Baton Rouge: Louisiana State University Press, 1965), p. 194.

Chapter 2: Amputation from the Trunk

[1] Ronald Sukenick, *Wallace Stevens: Musing the Obscure* (New York: New York University Press, 1967), p. 71.

[2] Sukenick, p. 72.

[3] Daniel Fuchs, *The Comic Spirit of Wallace Stevens* (Durham, N.C.: Duke University Press, 1963), p. 74.

[4] Edward Kessler, *Images of Wallace Stevens* (New Brunswick, N.J.: Rutgers University Press, 1972), p. 11.

[5] Riddel, p. 81.

[6] A. Walton Litz, *Introspective Voyager: The Poetic Development of Wallace Stevens* (New York: Oxford University Press, 1972), p. 120.

[7] Fuchs, p. 32.

[8] Fuchs, p. 34.

[9] Hi Simons, " 'The Comedian as the Letter C': Its Sense and Its Significance," *Southern Review*, 5 (1940), 454.

[10] Riddel, p. 102.

[11] Walt Whitman, "Crossing Brooklyn Ferry," in *Leaves of Grass*, ed. H. W. Blodgett and Sculley Bradley (New York: W. W. Norton, 1965), pp. 164–65.

[12] Riddel, p. 117.

[13] Kessler, p. 100.

[14] Riddel, p. 137.

[15] Susan B. Weston, *Wallace Stevens: An Introduction to the Poetry* (New York: Columbia University Press, 1977), pp. 71–72.

[16] Weston, p. 81.

[17] William Burney, *Wallace Stevens* (New York: Twayne, 1968), p. 151.

Chapter 3: Transport to Summer

[1] Helen Hennessy Vendler, *On Extended Wings: Wallace Stevens' Longer Poems* (Cambridge, Mass.: Harvard University Press, 1969), p. 207.

[2] For a discussion of the failure of "Notes" as a public document, see Robert J. Bertholf, "The Revolving Toward Myth: Stevens' 'Credences of Summer,' " *Bucknell Review*, 12 (1976), 208–29.

[3] Stephen E. Whicher, *Freedom and Fate: An Inner Life of Ralph Waldo Emerson* (Philadelphia: University of Pennsylvania Press, 1966), p. 36.

[4] *The Letters of William James and Theodore Fluornoy*, ed. Robert C. Le Clair (Madison: University of Wisconsin Press, 1966), p. 73. Emerson had written that the Civil War "is welcome to the Southerner; a chivalrous sport to him, like hunting, and suits his semi-civilized condition" (CWE XI 304).

[5] *The Letters of James and Fluornoy*, p. 73.

[6] This letter is cited in Ralph Barton Perry, *The Thought and Character of William James* (Cambridge, Mass.: Harvard University Press, 1948), p. 246.

[7] Fuchs, p. 157.

[8] James Baird, *The Dome and the Rock: Structure in the Poetry of Wallace Stevens* (Baltimore, Md.: Johns Hopkins University Press, 1968), p. 141.

[9] Curiously, the image of the theater in a context of war appeared twenty-six years earlier in the eighth of Stevens' "Lettres d'un Soldat":

> In a theatre, full of tragedy,
> The stage becomes an atmosphere
> Of seeping rose—banal machine
> In an appointed repertoire . . .
>
> (OP 15)

In "Repetitions," the "banal machine" becomes an ironic image for the modern heart of man, "Like a machine left running, and running down" (CP 306).

[10] Vendler, p. 206.

[11] Fuchs, p. 169.

[12] Fuchs, pp. 171–72.

[13] Fuchs, p. 177.

[14] Riddel, p. 211.

[15] Fuchs, p. 189.

[16] This and other references to *Varieties* in this chapter are not included in McDermott, *The Writings of William James*; pages cited refer to the Modern Library edition of *The Varieties of Religious Experience* (New York: Modern Library, 1936.)

[17] The passages cited here were part of the original paragraph James wrote to introduce his Gifford Lectures on natural religion. The paragraph was not included when the lectures were collected into *The Varieties of Religious Experience*. It is cited in Ralph Barton Perry, p. 258.

[18] J. Dennis Huston, " 'Credences of Summer': An Analysis," *Modern Philology* 67 (1970), p. 265.

[19] Vendler, p. 234.

[20] Huston, p. 271.
[21] Riddel, p. 222.

Chapter 4: In Winter's Nick

[1] Merle Brown, *Wallace Stevens: The Poem as Act* (Detroit, Mich.: Wayne State University, 1970), p. 175.
[2] Whicher, pp. 154–55.
[3] Whicher, p. 171.
[4] *The Correspondence of Emerson and Carlyle*, ed. Joseph Slater (New York: Columbia University Press, 1964), p. 540.
[5] J. Hillis Miller, *Poets of Reality* (Cambridge, Mass.: Harvard University Press, 1965), p. 270.
[6] Alfred North Whitehead, *Modes of Thought* (New York: Free Press, 1966), p. 3.
[7] Whitehead, p. 2.
[8] Whitehead, p. 3.
[9] Riddel, p. 225.
[10] Vendler, p. 269.
[11] Vendler, p. 249.
[12] Vendler, p. 269.
[13] Donald Davie, "The Auroras of Autumn," in *The Achievement of Wallace Stevens*, ed. Ashley Brown (Philadelphia: J. B. Lippincott, 1962), p. 167.
[14] Vendler, p. 258.
[15] Bloom, p. 279.
[16] Davie, p. 177.
[17] Brown, p. 195.
[18] Brown, p. 196.
[19] Vendler, p. 269.
[20] Vendler, pp. 269–70.
[21] Bloom, p. 306.
[22] Bloom, p. 306.
[23] Brown, p. 201.
[24] Riddel, p. 260.
[25] Vendler, p. 273.
[26] Brown, p. 204.
[27] Bloom, p. 335.

Chapter 5: Toward Stillness

[1] Riddel, p. 243.
[2] Riddel, p. 248.
[3] Doggett, pp. 5–6.
[4] Riddel, p. 254.
[5] Brown, p. 186.
[6] Sukenick, p. 195.
[7] Riddel, p. 243.
[8] Riddel, p. 250.
[9] Vendler, pp. 311–12.
[10] Vendler, p. 309.

WORKS CONSULTED

Primary Texts: Ralph Waldo Emerson

The Complete Works of Ralph Waldo Emerson. 12 vols. Concord edition. Boston: Houghton, Mifflin, 1904.

The Journals and Miscellaneous Notebooks of Ralph Waldo Emerson. 16 vols. Ed. William Gilman et al. Cambridge, Mass.: Harvard University Press, 1960.

The Letters of Ralph Waldo Emerson. 6 vols. Ed. Ralph Rusk. New York: Columbia University Press, 1939.

The Correspondence of Emerson and Carlyle. Ed. Joseph Slater. New York: Columbia University Press, 1964.

Primary Texts: William James

The Writings of William James: A Comprehensive Edition. Ed. John J. McDermott. Chicago: University of Chicago Press, 1977.

The Varieties of Religious Experience: A Study in Human Nature. New York: Modern Library, 1936.

The Letters of William James. 2 vols. Ed. Henry James. Boston: Atlantic Monthly Press, 1969.

The Letters of William James and Theodore Fluornoy. Ed. Robert C. Le Clair. Madison: University of Wisconsin Press, 1966.

Primary Texts: Wallace Stevens

The Collected Poems of Wallace Stevens. New York: Alfred A. Knopf, 1954.

Letters of Wallace Stevens. Ed. Holly Stevens. New York: Alfred A. Knopf, 1966.

The Necessary Angel: Essays on Reality and the Imagination. New York: Vintage Books, 1957.

Opus Posthumous. Ed. Samuel French Morse. New York: Alfred A. Knopf, 1951.

Secondary Sources: Ralph Waldo Emerson

Carpenter, Frederic Ives. *Emerson Handbook.* New York: Hendricks House, 1953.

————. "Points of Comparison Between Emerson and William James." *New England Quarterly*, 2 (1929), 458–74.

Eberhart, Richard. "Emerson and Wallace Stevens." *Literary Review*, 7 (1963), 51–71.

Hopkins, Vivian C. *Spires of Form: A Study of Emerson's Aesthetic Theory.* Cambridge, Mass.: Harvard University Press, 1951.

Huggard, William Allen. *Emerson and the Problem of War and Peace.* Diss. Iowa City: University of Iowa Humanistic Studies, 1938.

Konvitz, Milton R., and Stephen E. Whicher, eds. *Emerson: A Collection of Critical Essays.* Englewood Cliffs, N.J.: Prentice-Hall, 1962.

Levin, David, ed. *Emerson: Prophecy, Metamorphosis, and Influence.* New York: Columbia University Press, 1975.

Lindeman, Eduard C. "Emerson's Pragmatic Mood." *American Scholar*, 16 (1946–1947), 57–64.

Paul, Sherman. *Emerson's Angle of Vision: Man and Nature in American Experience.* Cambridge, Mass.: Harvard University Press, 1952.

Rountree, Thomas J., ed. *Critics on Emerson.* Coral Gables, Fla.: University of Miami Press, 1973.

Rusk, Ralph L. *The Life of Ralph Waldo Emerson.* New York: Charles Scribner's Sons, 1949.

Wagenknecht, Edward. *Ralph Waldo Emerson: Portrait of a Balanced Soul.* New York: Oxford University Press, 1974.

Whicher, Stephen E. *Freedom and Fate: An Inner Life of Ralph Waldo Emerson.* Philadelphia: University of Pennsylvania Press, 1966.

Secondary Sources: William James

Allen, Gay Wilson. *William James: A Biography.* New York: Viking Press, 1967.

Brennan, Bernard P. *William James.* New York: Twayne, 1968.

Carpenter, Frederic Ives. "William James and Emerson." *American Literature*, 11 (1939), 39–57.

Perry, Ralph Barton. *The Thought and Character of William James.* 2 vols. Boston: Little, Brown, 1935.

Rorty, Richard. *Consequences of Pragmatism.* Minneapolis, Minn.: University of Minnesota Press, 1982.

Wild, John. *The Radical Empiricism of William James.* New York: Doubleday, 1969.

Secondary Sources: Wallace Stevens

Baird, James. *The Dome and the Rock: Structure in the Poetry of Wallace Stevens.* Baltimore, Md.: Johns Hopkins University Press, 1968.

Benamou, Michel. *Wallace Stevens and the Symbolist Imagination.* Princeton, N.J.: Princeton University Press, 1972.

Bertholf, Robert J. "Renewing the Set: Wallace Stevens' 'The Auroras of Autumn.'" *Forum,* 17 (1976), 37–45.

———. "The Revolving Toward Myth: Stevens' 'Credences of Summer.'" *Bucknell Review,* 12 (1976), 208–29.

Bevis, William. "Metaphor in Wallace Stevens." *Shenandoah,* 15 (1964), 35–48.

Bloom, Harold. "The Central Man: Emerson, Whitman, Wallace Stevens." *Massachusetts Review,* 7 (1966), 23–42.

———. *Wallace Stevens: The Poems of Our Climate.* Ithaca, N.Y.: Cornell University Press, 1976.

Borroff, Marie, ed. *Wallace Stevens: A Collection of Critical Essays.* Englewood Cliffs, N.J.: Prentice-Hall, 1963.

Brown, Ashley, and Robert S. Haller, eds. *The Achievement of Wallace Stevens.* Philadelphia: J. B. Lippincott, 1962.

Brown, Merle. "Concordia Discors in the Poetry of Wallace Stevens." *American Literature,* 34 (1962), 246–69.

———. *Wallace Stevens: The Poem as Act.* Detroit, Mich.: Wayne State University Press, 1970.

Burney, William. *Wallace Stevens.* New York: Twayne, 1968.

Burnshaw, Stanley. "Turmoil in the Middle Ground." *New Masses,* 17 (1935), 41–42.

Buttel, Robert. *Wallace Stevens: The Making of Harmonium.* Princeton, N.J.: Princeton University Press, 1967.

Davie, Donald. "The Auroras of Autumn." *The Achievement of Wallace Stevens.* Ashley Brown, ed. Philadelphia, Pa.: J. B. Lippincott, 1962.

Doggett, Frank. *Stevens' Poetry of Thought.* Baltimore, Md.: Johns Hopkins University Press, 1968.

Edelstein, J. M. *Wallace Stevens: A Descriptive Bibliography.* Pittsburgh, Pa.: University of Pittsburgh Press, 1973.

Ellman, Richard. "Wallace Stevens' Ice-Cream." *Kenyon Review,* 19 (1957), 89–105.

Enck, John J. *Wallace Stevens: Images and Judgments.* Carbondale: Southern Illinois University Press, 1964.

Frye, Northrup. "The Realistic Oriole: A Study of Wallace Stevens." *Hudson Review,* 10 (1957), 353–70.

Fuchs, Daniel. *The Comic Spirit of Wallace Stevens.* Durham, N.C.: Duke University Press, 1963.

Gaskins, Avery F. "The Concept of Correspondence in the Works of Wallace Stevens and Ralph Waldo Emerson." *West Virginia University Philological Papers,* 15 (1966), 62–69.

Gregory, Horace. "An Examination of Wallace Stevens in a Time of War." *Accent*, 3 (1942), 57–61.

Heringman, Bernard. "Two Worlds and Epiphany." *Bard Review*, 2 (1948), 156–59.

Huston, J. Dennis. " 'Credences of Summer': An Analysis." *Modern Philology*, 67 (1970), 263–72.

Jarrell, Randall. "The Collected Poems of Wallace Stevens." *Yale Review*, 44 (1955), 340–53.

Kessler, Edward. *Images of Wallace Stevens*. New Brunswick, N.J.: Rutgers University Press, 1972.

Lawler, Justus George. "The Poet, the Metaphysician and the Desire for God." *Downside Review*, 84 (1966), 288–304.

Litz, A. Walton. *Introspective Voyager: The Poetic Development of Wallace Stevens*. New York: Oxford University Press, 1972.

MacCaffrey, Isabel G. "The Other Side of Silence: 'Credences of Summer' as an Example." *Modern Language Quarterly*, 30 (1969), 417–38.

Martz, Louis. "Wallace Stevens: The World as Meditation." *Yale Review*, 47 (1958), 517–36.

Middlebrook, Diane Wood. *Walt Whitman and Wallace Stevens*. Ithaca, N.Y.: Cornell University Press, 1974.

Morris, Adalaide Kirby. *Wallace Stevens: Imagination and Faith*. Princeton, N.J.: Princeton University Press, 1974.

Morse, Samuel French. *Wallace Stevens: Poetry as Life*. New York: Pegasus, 1970.

Mulqueen, James E. "Wallace Stevens: Radical Transcendentalist." *Midwest Quarterly*, 11 (1970), 329–40.

Nasser, Eugene Paul. *Wallace Stevens: An Anatomy of Figuration*. Philadelphia: University of Pennsylvania Press, 1965.

O'Connor, William Van. *The Shaping Spirit: A Study of Wallace Stevens*. Chicago: Henry Regnery, 1950.

Pack, Robert. *Wallace Stevens: An Approach to His Poetry and Thought*. New Brunswick, N.J.: Rutgers University Press, 1958.

Pearce, Roy Harvey, and J. Hillis Miller, eds. *The Act of the Mind: Essays on the Poetry of Wallace Stevens*. Baltimore, Md.: Johns Hopkins University Press, 1965.

Perlis, Alan. *Wallace Stevens: A World of Transforming Shapes*. Lewisburg, Pa.: Bucknell University Press, 1976.

Peterson, Margaret L. W. "*Harmonium* and William James." *Southern Review*, 7 (1971), 658–82.

Riddel, Joseph. *The Clairvoyant Eye: The Poetry and Politics of Wallace Stevens*. Baton Rouge: Louisiana State University Press, 1965.

Simons, Hi. " 'The Comedian as the Letter C': Its Sense and Its Significance." *Southern Review*, 5 (1940), 453–68.
Stern, Herbert J. *Wallace Stevens: Art of Uncertainty*. Ann Arbor: The University of Michigan Press, 1966.
Sukenick, Ronald. *Wallace Stevens: Musing the Obscure*. New York: New York University Press, 1967.
Vendler, Helen Hennessy. *On Extended Wings: Wallace Stevens' Longer Poems*. Cambridge, Mass.: Harvard University Press, 1969.
Walsh, Thomas F. *Concordance to the Poetry of Wallace Stevens*. University Park: Pennsylvania State University Press, 1963.
Watts, Harold H. "Wallace Stevens and the Rock of Summer." *Kenyon Review*, 14 (1952), 122–40.
Weston, Susan B. *Wallace Stevens: An Introduction to the Poetry*. New York: Columbia University Press, 1977.
Young, David P. "A Skeptical Music: Stevens and Santayana." *Criticism*, 7 (1965), 263–83.

General Works
Bloom, Harold. *Agon: Towards a Theory of Revisionism*. New York: Oxford University Press, 1982.
Bradley, Sculley, Richmond Croom Beatty, and E. Hudson Long, eds. *The American Tradition in Literature*. Shorter Edition. New York: W. W. Norton, 1974.
DeMott, Robert J. and Sanford E. Marovitz, eds. *Artful Thunder: Versions of the Romantic Tradition in American Literature in Honor of Howard P. Vincent*. Kent, Ohio: Kent State University Press, 1975.
Hofstadter, Richard. *Social Darwinism in American Thought*. New York: George Braziller, 1955.
Kermode, Frank. *The Sense of an Ending: Studies in the Theory of Fiction*. London: Oxford University Press, 1966.
Miller, J. Hillis. *Poets of Reality*. Cambridge, Mass.: Harvard University Press, 1965.
Otto, Rudolf. *The Idea of the Holy*. Trans. John W. Harvey. London: Oxford University Press, 1958.
Pearce, Roy Harvey. *The Continuity of American Poetry*. Princeton, N.J.: Princeton University Press, 1961.
Peckham, Morse. *Man's Rage for Chaos: Biology, Behavior and the Arts*. Philadelphia: Chilton, 1965.
———. *Romanticism and Behavior*. Columbia, S.C.: University of South Carolina Press, 1976.

Waggoner, Hyatt H. *American Poets from the Puritans to the Present.* Boston: Houghton Mifflin, 1968.

Whitehead, Alfred North. *Modes of Thought.* New York: Free Press, 1966.

INDEX

"Academic Discourse in Havana," 5, 60

Adagia, 6, 15, 16, 37, 165, 174

"The American Scholar" (Emerson), 20, 25, 38, 45, 57, 66, 81, 92, 159

Amiel: *Journal in Time*, 112; mentioned, 114

Anderson, Sherwood, 145

"Asides on the Oboe," 13, 16, 81

The Auroras of Autumn, 120, 127

"The Auroras of Autumn," 120, 121, 126, 127–40, 141, 145, 156

"Autumn Refrain," 60

Baird, James, 99

"Bantams in Pine-Woods," 45

Bloom, Harold, 3, 23, 138, 142, 154

Boston Evening Transcript, 94

Brook Farm, 55

Brown, John, 89

Brown, Merle, 121, 141, 147, 154, 167

Burney, William, 84

Carlyle, Thomas, 123

Carpenter, Frederic, 2, 91

Center, theory of man at, 2, 22–28, 145

Chaos, 3, 36–38

Christianity, 22, 26, 45, 48, 82–83, 90, 93, 103, 104, 109, 118, 122, 123, 173, 174

Church, Barbara, 166

Church, Henry, 96

"Circles" (Emerson), 5, 65, 145

Civil War, 89–92, 94, 181n

Coleridge, Samuel, 15

"The Comedian as the Letter C," 39, 50–58, 64, 132

Communism, 5

"Credences of Summer," 109, 113–20, 121, 124, 127, 128, 131, 135, 137, 141, 145, 151, 158, 162

Darwinian era, 50

Davie, Donald, 131, 139

"Description Without Place," 100, 113

"The Divinity School Address" (Emerson), 104

Doggett, Frank, 3, 164

"Domination of Black," 39–40

"Dutch Graves in Bucks County," 97–98, 101

"Earthy Anecdote," 30, 42

"Effects of Analogy," 126

Eliade, Mircea, 117

Eliot, T. S., 26

Emancipation Proclamation, 89

Emerson, Ralph Waldo: on action, 1; as an aging man, 121–24; image of center in, 22–28; and the central man, 23, 25, 72, 82; and chaos, 3; and Christianity, 90, 104, 122, 123; and the Civil War, 89–92, 181n; and notion of decreation, 24; and notion of eternal cause, 6; and evil, 90; image of eye in, 146; and fate, 90, 91; and freedom, 163; on history, 3–4; on language, 16, 32–33; on metaphor, 16; and the Mexican War, 89, 91, 94; on the poet's function, 16, 85; relation to pragmatism, 11–12; and process, 4–5; and the scholar, 117, 161; and the scholar-poet, 24, 38–39, 60, 66–67, 139, 156; and slavery, 90, 91; on subject-object relationship, 29–35; and tragedy, 90–91; and transparent eyeball image, 13, 82, 111, 161; on truth, 14–15, 20; and visionary moments, 111. *See also individual Emerson titles*

"The Emperor of Ice-Cream," 115

189